get
your
life
back

get
your
life
back

EVERYDAY PRACTICES
FOR A WORLD GONE MAD

JOHN ELDREDGE

NELSON
BOOKS

An Imprint of Thomas Nelson

Published in Nashville, Tennessee, by Nelson Books, an imprint of Thomas Nelson. Nelson Books and Thomas Nelson are registered trademarks of HarperCollins Christian Publishing, Inc.

Published in association with Yates & Yates, www.yates2.com.

Thomas Nelson titles may be purchased in bulk for educational, business, fund-raising, or sales promotional use. For information, please e-mail SpecialMarkets@ThomasNelson.com.

Unless otherwise noted, Scripture quotations are taken from the Holy Bible, New International Version®, NIV®. Copyright © 1973, 1978, 1984, 2011 by Biblica, Inc.® Used by permission of Zondervan. All rights reserved worldwide. www.Zondervan.com. The "NIV" and "New International Version" are trademarks registered in the United States Patent and Trademark Office by Biblica, Inc.®

Scripture quotations marked THE MESSAGE are from *The Message*. Copyright © by Eugene H. Peterson 1993, 1994, 1995, 1996, 2000, 2001, 2002. Used by permission of NavPress. All rights reserved. Represented by Tyndale House Publishers, Inc.

Scripture quotations marked NLT are from the Holy Bible, New Living Translation. © 1996, 2004, 2007, 2013, 2015 by Tyndale House Foundation. Used by permission of Tyndale House Publishers, Inc., Carol Stream, Illinois 60188. All rights reserved.

ISBN 978-1-4002-0867-8 (eBook)
ISBN 978-1-4002-0866-1 (HC)
ISBN 978-1-4002-1921-6 (IE)
ISBN 978-1-4002-2914-7 (TP)

Library of Congress Control Number: 2019953528

Printed in the United States of America

21 22 23 24 25 LSC 10 9 8 7 6 5 4 3 2 1

For Brian Hampton, friend and comrade since
the beginning. We'll see you soon, pal.

May the Son of God, who is already formed in you, grow in you, so that for you he will become immeasurable, and that in you he will become laughter, exultation, the fullness of joy which no one can take from you.

—ISAAC OF STELLA

CONTENTS

CONTENTS

Introduction

THE RESCUE

This book has a remarkable story.

I wrote the manuscript in 2019, concerned about the beleaguered condition of the human soul in the world at that time. We released the book in February 2020—just days before the COVID-19 pandemic rolled across the globe. No one of course knew what was coming, but everything I had written took on a new urgency. Now, after all the lockdowns, quarantines, and chronic losses of everything that makes for happy daily living, the need to get our lives back could not be greater.

We have all passed through global trauma together. You can see the effects in our mental fragmentation, weariness, irritability, and the lingering anxiety. Our souls need some serious, loving care. In his kindness, Jesus orchestrated the timing of this book, and it is proving a rescue and a delight to hundreds of thousands of people. Every word here seems designed to lift us out of a post-pandemic world.

For this is how my original introduction began . . .

————————

There's a madness to our moment, and we need to name it for the lunacy it is. Because it's taking our lives hostage.

First, there's the blistering pace of life.

I texted friends an announcement that was really important to me; they replied with little thumbs-up emojis. I think to myself, *That's it—you can't even answer a text with a* text? Email felt so efficient when it replaced the letter; texting seemed like rocket fuel when it came along. But it didn't make our lives more spacious; we simply had to keep up. Now we're living at the speed of the swipe and the "like," moving so fast through our days that typing a single sentence feels cumbersome. Everyone I talk to says they feel busier than ever. My musician friends aren't playing much anymore; my gardening friends don't have time to plant; I currently have eight books I've started to read, and I haven't made it past the first chapter in any of them.

We've been sucked into a pace of life nobody's enjoying.

Then there's the deluge of media coming at us in a sort of mesmerizing digital spell.

We're spending three hours a day using apps on our phones, ten hours viewing media, consuming enough information each week to crash a laptop (!).[1] We talk about unplugging, but we're enchanted—by the endless social media circus of love and hatred, the vapid, alarming, sensational, and unforgivable. We're snagged by every new notification. And while we've always had our individual struggles and heartbreaks to deal with, now we have the tragedies of the entire world delivered to us hourly on our mobile devices.

This is all very hard on the soul. Traumatizing, in fact. Exposure to traumatic events can traumatize us, and we're getting lots of it in our feed.[2] It's like we've been swept into the gravitational field of a digital black hole that is sucking our lives from us.

So there's all that. But everybody's talking about that. What got my attention was what was happening to me *as a person.*

I found myself flinching when a friend texted and asked for some time. I didn't want to open email for fear of the demands I'd find there. I had a shorter and shorter fuse in traffic. I felt numb to tragic news reports. It made me wonder—*am I becoming a less-loving person?* I had little capacity for relationships and the things that bring me life—a walk in the woods, dinner with friends, a cold plunge in a mountain lake. When I did steal a moment for something life-giving, I was so distracted I couldn't enjoy it.

Then I realized—it wasn't a failure of love or compassion. These were symptoms of a soul pushed too hard, strung out, haggard, fried. My soul just can't do life at the speed of smartphones. But I was asking it to; everybody's asking theirs to.

I'm guessing you've experienced something similar. It's likely why you've picked up this book—your soul is looking for something. Are you aware of what it is? How would you score your soul these days:

Are you happy most of the time?

How often do you feel lighthearted?

Are you excited about your future?

Do you feel deeply loved?

When was the last time you felt carefree?

I know, it's not even fair to ask. Our souls are bleary, seared, smeared. Still able to love, yes; still able to hope and dream. But at the end of any given day, most people come home in a state of exhaustion. Numb on our good days, fried more often than we admit. "I feel all thin, sort of stretched," as Bilbo Baggins said, "like butter that has been scraped over too much bread."[3]

The world has gone completely mad, and it's trying to take our souls with it.

Now, if we had more of God, that would really help. We could draw upon his love and strength, his wisdom and resilience. After all, God is the fountain of life (Psalm 36:9). If we had more of his lavish life bubbling up in us, it would be a rescue in this soul-scorching hour.

But this frantic, volatile world constantly wilts the soul, dries it out like a raisin, making it almost impossible to *receive* the life God is pouring forth.

That's called a double bind.

I tried to find more of God, knowing if I only had a greater measure of his life in me, I'd be able to navigate this rough terrain. I was practicing the usual stuff—prayer, worship, scripture, sacrament.

But still I felt . . . I don't know . . . shallow somehow. Sipping God with teaspoons, not drinking great gulps; wading, not swimming. My soul felt like a shallow rain puddle. But I know the soul isn't a shallow puddle at all; it's deep and vast, capable of symphonies and heroic courage. I wanted to be living from those deep places, but I felt trapped in the shoals.

It's no coincidence that one of the most important books on our world, and what technology is doing to us, is called *The Shallows: What the Internet Is Doing to Our Brains*. We're losing our ability to focus and pay attention longer than a few moments. We live at the depth of the text, the swipe, the "like."[4] This isn't just an intellectual problem; it's a spiritual crisis. It's pretty hard to hear "deep calling unto deep"[5] when we're forced into the shallows of our own hearts and souls by this frenetic world.

Jesus heard even my surface prayers; he came to my rescue and began to lead me into a number of helps and practices, what I would call graces. Simple things, like a One Minute Pause, that were accessible and surprising in their power to restore. Learning "benevolent detachment"—the ability to let things go. Allowing for some transition in my day, instead of just blasting from one thing to the next. Drinking in the beauty God was providing in quiet moments. My soul began to recover, feel better, do better—however you want to describe it. I began to enjoy my life with God so much more; I was finally experiencing the "more" of him I'd been wanting so much. I began to get my life back.

Then I connected the dots. . . .

God *wants* to come to us and restore our lives. He really does.

But if our soul is not well, it's almost impossible to receive him. Dry, scorched ground can't absorb the very rain it needs.

As C. S. Lewis explained, "The soul is but a hollow which God fills."[6] In place of *hollow* I like the word *vessel*, something beautiful and artistic. Our souls are exquisite vessels created by God for him to saturate. I picture the round, curved basin at the top of an elegant fountain, with water spilling down all sides, running over with unceasing life. Wasn't that the promise? "As Scripture has said, rivers of living water will flow from within them" (John 7:38).

And so it follows that if we can receive help for restoring and renewing our weary, besieged souls, we'll enjoy the fruits (which are many and wonderful) of happy souls and also be able to receive more of God (which is even more wonderful). We'll find the vibrancy and resiliency we crave as human beings, living waters welling up from deep within. And then—we'll get our lives back!

But the process needs to be accessible and sustainable. We've all tried exercise, diets, Bible study programs that began with vim and verve but over time got shoved to the side, lost in the chaos. I have a gym membership; I rarely use it. There are those books I haven't finished, loads of podcasts too. Rest assured—the graces I am offering here are within reach of a normal life. I think you'll find them simple, sustainable, and refreshing.

God wants to strengthen and renew your soul; Jesus longs to give you more of himself. Come, you weary and heavy laden. "Are you tired? Worn out? Burned out on religion? Come to me. Get away with me and you'll recover your life . . . and you'll learn to live freely and lightly" (Matthew 11:28–30 THE MESSAGE). You can get your life back; you can live freely and lightly. The world may be harsh, but God is gentle; he knows what your life is like. What we need to do is put ourselves in places that allow us to receive his help. Let me show you how.

one

THE ONE MINUTE PAUSE

I'm pretty sure a lion came through in the night. Our horses are live wires this morning—racing back and forth across their pasture, necks arched, tails high, snorting. Something put them on high alert.

My wife and I currently have two horses. One is a Paint (sometimes called a Pinto), a beautiful brown-and-white-spotted horse with white mane and black tail. If you saw the western classic *Silverado*, Kevin Costner rode a Paint in that film. The Plains Indians loved the look of Paints so much they would literally paint their ordinary horses to look spotted.[1]

Our other horse is a solid brown bay, black mane and tail, with a coat so rich and glossy it looks like a beaver pelt. We used to have eight ponies altogether, but over time as our sons moved away, we trimmed our herd down to a more manageable size. Still, sometimes even caring for two feels like more than we've got room for.

Horses are powerful, magnificent creatures, but they don't see themselves that way; in their inner life they feel *vulnerable*. They are, after all, prey animals like elk and deer, that developed their view of the world and their survival skills on the plains of North America and Europe, running from large animals trying to eat them. In the Late Pleistocene, the plains were hunting grounds for huge lions bigger than an African lion, several types of cheetahs, terrible giant ground sloths, dire wolves, voracious short-faced bears, and a host of other high-octane predators. Horses learned their nervous ways in a very rough playground; there's a whole lot of "flight" in their "fight or flight" response.

Come summer we keep our ponies at our cabin out in the western Colorado sage. There are all sorts of predators here—packs of coyotes, black bears, bobcats, lynx, and mountain lions. Lots of lions. I had a horse blow up under me because he simply smelled lion. There was no lion there, but the males mark their territories with their scent. The horse I was riding got one whiff and exploded, leaving me behind in a pile.

Predators hunt under cover of darkness; from the horse's point of view, nighttime calls for high vigilance. Come morning we often need to settle them down before we attempt a ride, so we groom them and do some "ground work." At some point in their connection with us—once they're feeling safe and secure—they let out this wonderful sigh. Out of those large nostrils comes a big, deep, long breath. Their muscles relax; their heads lower. They have switched off hypervigilant mode. I love it when they do that; you're looking for that sigh when you're working with horses.

We humans make that sigh, too, when we feel settled and in a good place.

I'll bet you've experienced that sigh yourself. You get home from a long day, kick off your shoes, grab something to drink, maybe a bag of chips, collapse into your favorite chair, pull a comfy throw over you. Then comes that wonderful sigh. Sometimes we experience it in moments of beauty—sitting on the beach at sunset, pausing by a lake so still it looks like glass. We're comforted by the beauty and sigh. Everything seems right. Sometimes that deep, long exhale comes when we remember a truth precious to us. We read a verse reminding us how much God loves us, and we lean back and sigh as our soul settles back into the comfort of it. I did so just this morning.

It's a good sign, however it comes. It means we're coming down from hypervigilance mode ourselves.

FIGHT OR FLIGHT

We, too, live in a world that triggers our souls into vigilance far too often. The complexity of modern life is mind-boggling: the constantly changing social terrain of what's appropriate, the level of trauma we navigate in people's lives. The typical sounds of a city trigger adrenaline responses in us all day long; that deep throbbing bass *whump* coming from the car four lanes over, the one you feel all through your body, is not that different from the sound of

3

distant artillery. Thanks to the smartphone and the web, you are confronted on a daily basis with more information than any previous generation had to deal with! And it's not just information; it's the suffering of the entire planet, in minute detail, served up on your feed daily. Add to this the pace at which most of us are required to live our lives. It leaves very little room for that sigh and the experiences that bring it.

We live in a spiritual and emotional state equivalent to horses on the plains during the Late Pleistocene.

This morning I can't tell whether my soul is more in fight or flight. But I do know this—I don't like the state I'm in. I didn't sleep well last night (one of the many consequences of living in a hypercharged world), and after I finally conked out, I overslept, woke up late, and ever since I've felt behind on everything.

I rushed through breakfast, dashed out the door to get to some meetings, and now I'm rattled. I don't like that feeling, and I don't like the consequences. When I'm rattled, I'm easily irritated with people. I didn't have the patience to listen to what my wife was trying to say this morning. I find it hard to hear from God, and I don't like feeling untethered from him.

I notice now in my rattled state that I want to eat something fatty and sugary; I want something that's going to make me feel better *now*. When we're unsettled, unnerved, unhinged, it's human nature to seek a sense of equilibrium, stability, and I find myself wondering—how many addictions begin here, with just wanting a little comfort? Get out of the rattled place and soothe ourselves with "a little something?"

We live in a crazy-making world. So much stimulation rushes at us with such unrelenting fury, we are overstimulated most of the time. Things that nourish us—a lingering conversation, a leisurely stroll through the park, time to savor both making and then enjoying dinner—these are being lost at an alarming rate; we simply don't have room for them. Honestly, I think most people live their daily lives along a spectrum from slightly rattled to completely fried as their normal state of being.

In the late morning, I finally do what I should have from the beginning—I pause, get quiet, settle down. I give myself permission to simply pause, a little breathing room to come back to myself and God. My breathing returns to normal (I didn't even notice I was holding my breath). A little bit of space begins to clear around me. Suddenly, somewhere outside, someone has just fired up a leaf blower—one of the great pariahs of the human race, the enemy of all tranquility. My body tenses, the stress returns, and because I'm paying attention, I see for myself how the constant stimulation of our chaotic world causes us to live in a state of hypervigilance.

Notice—are your muscles relaxed right now or tense? Is your breathing deep and relaxed, or are you taking short, shallow breaths? Are you able to read this leisurely, or do you feel you need to get through it quickly? Most of the day we simply plow through a myriad of diverse tasks, checking boxes, "getting stuff done." It frazzles the soul, so we look to all our "comforters" to calm down. But I know my salvation is not in the frappuccino nor the fudge. So I close the window against the screams of the leaf blower and return to a practice that's become an absolute lifesaver:

The One Minute Pause.

I simply take sixty seconds to be still and let everything go.

As I enter the pause, I begin with release. I let it all go—the meetings, what I know is coming next, the fact I'm totally behind on everything, all of it. I simply let it go. I pray, *Jesus—I give everyone and everything to you.* I keep repeating it until I feel like I'm actually releasing and detaching. *I give everyone and everything to you, God.* All I'm trying to accomplish right now is a little bit of soul-space. I'm not trying to fix anything or figure anything out. I'm not trying to release everything perfectly or permanently. That takes a level of maturity most of us haven't found. But I can let it go for sixty seconds. (That's the brilliance of the pause—all we are asking ourselves to do is let go for sixty seconds.) And as I do, even as I say it out loud—*I give everyone and everything to you*—my soul cooperates a good bit. I'm settling down.

I even sigh, that good sigh.

Then I ask for more of God: *Jesus—I need more of you; fill me with more of you, God. Restore our union; fill me with your life.*

You'll be surprised what a minute can do for you. Even more so as you get practiced at it. Honestly, you can do this pause nearly anytime, anywhere—in your car, on the train, after you get off your phone. I know it seems small, but we have to start somewhere. This pause is accessible; it's doable.

As David wrote in the Psalms, "I have calmed and quieted

myself" (131:2). Or, "I've cultivated a quiet heart." I wonder how many people in your office, your gym, your daily commute could say they've cultivated a quiet heart? What we assume is a normal lifestyle is absolute insanity to the God-given nature of our heart and soul. Broad is the path that leads to destruction, and many there are who travel it.

Nonetheless, this is the world we live in, raise our kids in, navigate our careers in, and so we need to find things that are simple and accessible to begin to take back our souls. The One Minute Pause is within reach. The practice itself is wonderful, and it opens space in your soul for God to meet you there.

The desert fathers of the third and fourth century were a courageous, ragtag group, followers of Jesus who fled the madness of their world to seek a life of beauty and simplicity with God in the silent desert. For they saw the world as "a shipwreck from which every man has to swim for their life."[2] And think of it: they had no cell phones, no Internet, no media per se, not one automobile, Starbucks, or leaf blower. The news that came their way was local; they did not carry the burdens of every community in the world. They walked everywhere they went. Therefore, they lived at the pace of *three miles an hour* (!). Yet they felt the world sucking the life out of them, and they decided to do something about it.

And so we who live in a far more insane hour and who want to find a better life in God ought to be the first to adopt a few practices that get us out of the madness and into a more settled way of living. Most of us would be happy simply to be a little less rattled.

GENTLE REMINDERS

We live most of our year in suburbia, in a small valley on the edge of our city. Years before suburban development crept in, a convent was established here by the Sisters of St. Francis. The abbey is a medley of beautiful sandstone buildings scattered through rolling grounds of pine and juniper. The sisters have the most lovely practice of solemnly ringing church bells first thing in the morning at six. These aren't the raucous bells that follow a wedding; these are slow, methodic rings: a call to prayer. They sound again in the evening at six. I love the resonance of old bells; they echo through our little valley like a summons out of the past. A call to prayer or silence. I decided to accept the call myself and let the bells be reminders to me to take the One Minute Pause.

A few years ago we took up the practice in our offices. At 10 a.m. and 2 p.m. every day, monastery "bells" ring out as a call to the staff to stop what they're doing, let it all go, and center ourselves in Christ again. I instituted the "corporate" practice because I noticed that I simply go from one thing to another to another, without pause, from morning till night. I finish a phone call and make another. I complete one email and plow through a dozen more. Before I can get through my inbox, I go find someone I need to meet with. There's no pause in my day, no sacred space at all. If God is going to get in, he's practically got to force his way. And I've noticed that God doesn't like to shout. He doesn't like to be forced to gymnastics to get our attention, no more than you like having to jump up and down to get your friend or spouse to notice you're in the room.

So I've seized the One Minute Pause as my sword against the madness. After I finish a phone call and before I start something else, I simply pause. When I pull into work in the morning and when I pull into my driveway in the evening, I pause. I literally lay my head down on my steering wheel and just pause, for one minute. It sounds almost too simple to be a practice that brings me more of God, but it's very effective. Because what it does is open up soul space, breathing room. And God is right there. Over time, the *cumulative* effect is even better. It's reshaping the pace of my day. It's training my soul to find God as an experience more common than rare. I feel better. I'm now treating people more kindly.

GIVING IT A TRY

The One Minute Pause can be used in many ways: for prayer or silence, to find your heart again, or to enjoy a moment of beauty. We'll develop this practice as we go along in this book. For now, here's a way to start:

Pick one or two moments in your day when you know you are least likely to be interrupted. One of those for me is when I pull into the driveway at the end of the day. I don't have to leap from the car; I can take a moment. I turn the engine off, sometimes lay my head down on the steering wheel, and just breathe. I try to let go of the day.

It will help if you set your phone alarm to remind you. Pick a notification sound that is gracious, not adrenaline producing ("Bell," or better "Silk." Not "Suspense" or "News Flash" for you iPhone users). You are not sounding an alarm; you are inviting your soul to a gracious pause.

I have developed an app called the One Minute Pause, to help you with this practice; it's beautiful, and I think will be of great service to you. You can find it for free in the app store. This is the beginning of a new way of living, one simple practice that opens the door to many others. Your soul is going to thank you.

two

BENEVOLENT DETACHMENT

I'm sitting on a bluff in the wild southwest corner of Wyoming, sweeping the horizon with my binoculars. The view up here is staggering—only sagebrush and coarse grasses for hundreds of miles in every direction; I can see the curve of the earth. It's going to be a hot August day. Heat waves are already shimmering in my view, making it hard to spot my quarry. Most folks would probably call these the badlands. Blistering in summer, freezing all winter, nearly always windy—but I come here because wild horses love this country. They feel safe out here.

There are still hundreds of herds of wild horses running through the American West, a fact that makes my soul happy. Wildness, open spaces, and animals living in utter freedom are all good for our humanity. Sometimes we need geography to usher our soul into spaciousness, lightheartedness. And so I've come.

A golden eagle is sitting only twenty yards downslope in front of me. Golden eagles are massive raptors, with seven-foot wingspans and the strength to carry off fawns and lambs. This one is perched on the edge of a cliff, scanning the alkaline landscape for prey. It's a perfect perch for him; with the updrafts coming up the bluff, all he has to do is spread his wings, step off, and he's gone. I can't believe he hasn't seen me. Maybe he has and simply doesn't care. I sigh with peace and happiness.

At dawn this morning I got in my truck, pointed myself north, and just . . . drove away. For a blissful week of solitude. No real plans: only my camping gear, fishing rod, and maps of the Wind River range, Yellowstone, and Montana. This is an unplanned, last-minute trip—something Jesus practically insisted on. Many moons have come and gone since I took time to get away, care for my soul, find God.

And I must tell you, it's an extraordinary feeling to have your world fading in the rearview mirror, nothing but an open road before you.

It's a practice Jesus himself cherished (minus the truck). I've always been intrigued by his ability to just up and walk away from his world. Right there in the opening chapter of Mark, with excitement building and crowds swelling all round him, Jesus disappears. He just . . . leaves.

> Very early in the morning, while it was still dark, Jesus got up, left the house and went off to a solitary place, where he prayed. Simon and his companions went to look for him, and when they

found him, they exclaimed: "Everyone is looking for you!" Jesus
replied, "Let us go somewhere else." (Mark 1:35–38)

Jesus models a freedom of heart I think every one of us would love
to have. His ability to disengage himself from his world is so alluring.

So, like a good disciple, I've done the same. Everyone is wanting
something from me, so I've followed my Master and . . . left. If I
wanted to see wild horses, I probably should have gotten here sooner,
but ever since I left home this morning, I've been moseying, stopping
to read those "points of historical interest" I usually blast by. It'll take
a few days to enter in, but already I can feel that exquisite condition
coming on—a rare, carefree lightheartedness.

ENTANGLED

Boy, oh boy, is it hard to disentangle from our world.

Before nature began its healing work here on this high plateau, I
had spent the previous twenty-four hours obsessing over a comment
someone made to me during a business meeting.

Honestly, it was only a simple observation on their part, shared
within a larger conversation. But the observation was about *me*, and
you know how that goes—it became the one thing in a twenty-minute
conversation I seized upon, like that chia seed caught between your
teeth. You can't think about anything else; your tongue searches it
out and hovers around it. Over time the quite simple, rather benign

remark has become filled with implication and all sorts of subterfuge as I wonder and worry and speculate over what this colleague meant. I think you know well the experience I'm talking about—somebody says something to you in passing, and later you find yourself wondering, then worrying, what they meant by it.

You're running late; you text a coworker or your boss a gentle explanation that your child woke up sick and you had to arrange for care before you left for work. All you receive back is a one-word reply: "Okay." What does it mean? Are they mad at you? They're probably mad at you; one word feels like they are. They didn't say, "Oh gosh, I'm so sorry; hope they are feeling better. Totally understand. No worries." But they may also be driving and not supposed to text, and one word was all they could manage to let you know it's okay. But all those possibilities play out in our minds, so we worry over subtext and intended meaning.

I don't think of myself as an obsessive person, but in looking back upon the conversation, the comment feels loaded—which leads me to wonder what the subtext was, which leads me to wonder about the subtext to *everything* this person said to me in the conversation. Which leads me to wonder what the subtext was to other conversations we've had and to emails received in the last month. Which leads me to wonder what the subtext is to our relationship, and have I been misinterpreting everything that has been taking place?! One small comment in a marketing meeting triggered an avalanche of speculation in me—speculation about motives, my leadership, the integrity of this relationship altogether.

Lord, help us.

Over the course of these very unhelpful twenty-four hours, every time I turned to Jesus to try to get some peace and orientation, he simply kept saying, *Give this to me. Release this to me. Give them to me.* And I was struck by how difficult that is, especially once we're really worked up in speculation, worry, genuine concern, or anxiety.

Jesus didn't offer interpretation; he didn't offer encouragement. Before I could do anything else, I needed to get out of the quagmire. I needed distance, breathing room. I needed his grace before I could even begin to reinterpret all that I'd been misinterpreting. When Peter began to sink into the Sea of Galilee, Jesus didn't offer perspective; he didn't pause to talk it through. He offered his hand to lift the drowning man out of the waves and back into the boat. Release first; interpretation later.

As I began to practice the smallest measure of release, the relief was almost immediate.

BENEVOLENT DETACHMENT

We are talking in this book about making room in our lives for God so that we might receive more of his wonderful self in us and, with that, the vibrancy and resiliency we crave as human beings. There are external ways we can do this, simple steps like the One Minute Pause. And there are internal ways we do this as well.

To make room for God to fill the vessel of our soul, we have to begin moving out some of the unnecessary clutter that continually accumulates there like the junk drawer in your kitchen. Everybody has a junk drawer, that black hole for car keys, pens, paper clips, gum, all the small flotsam and jetsam that accumulates over time. Our souls accumulate stuff, too, pulling it in like a magnet. And so Augustine said we must empty ourselves of all that fills us so that we may be filled with what we are empty of.[1] Over time I've found no better practice to help clear out my cluttered soul than the practice of benevolent detachment. The ability to let it go, walk away—not so much physically but emotionally, *soulfully*.

Allow me to explain. We are aiming for release, turning over into the hands of God whatever is burdening us *and leaving it there*. It's so easy to get caught up in the drama in unhealthy ways, and then we are unable to see clearly, set boundaries, respond freely. When this happens in relationships, psychologists call it enmeshment.

> Repeated exposure to enmeshed relationships can prevent the developing child from becoming aware of and knowing herself physically as well as emotionally. The lines between empathizing (identifying with and understanding another person's feelings or difficulties), and overidentifying (becoming enmeshed with another person) vanish.[2]

Mature adults have learned how to create a healthy distance between themselves and the thing they have become entangled with. Thus the word *detachment*. It means getting untangled, stepping out of the quagmire; it means peeling apart the Velcro by which this person, relationship, crisis, or global issue has attached itself to you. Or you to it. Detachment means getting some healthy distance. Social media overloads our empathy. So I use the word "benevolent" in referring to this necessary kind of detachment because we're not talking about cynicism or resignation. Benevolent means kindness. It means something done in love. Jesus invites us into a way of living where we are genuinely comfortable turning things over to him:

> Then Jesus said, "Come to me, all of you who are weary and carry heavy burdens, and I will give you rest. Take my yoke upon you. Let me teach you, because I am humble and gentle at heart, and you will find rest for your souls. For my yoke is easy to bear, and the burden I give you is light." (Matthew 11:28–30 NLT)
>
> Are you tired? Worn out? Burned out on religion? Come to me. Get away with me and you'll recover your life. I'll show you how to take a real rest. Walk with me and work with me—watch how I do it. Learn the unforced rhythms of grace. I won't lay anything heavy or ill-fitting on you. Keep company with me and you'll learn to live freely and lightly. (Matthew 11:28–30 THE MESSAGE)

Now, pay attention here—Jesus said there is a way "to live freely and *lightly*."

His dear friend Peter echoes the invitation later in the New Testament:

> Cast all your anxiety on him because he cares for you. (1 Peter 5:7)
>
> Live carefree before God; he is most careful with you. (1 Peter 5:7 The Message)

Carefree? The offer is a *carefree life?!* I love feeling carefree. Carefree is how I feel in the middle of vacation; it's how I feel now as I make my way through the wildlands, with nothing but an open road before me. People are desperately seeking the feeling of carefree. I think all our dissociative patterns are signs of it—the video games, the virtual reality craze, the chemicals we use to feel unburdened. You can see human beings trying to disentangle in the popularity of the helpful book *Boundaries*, which has sold millions of copies. We're looking for a way to take back some healthy detachment in our lives.

Notice the runaway hit song "Let It Go" from the 2013 Disney movie *Frozen*. You had to be in an underground cave to miss it. Young and not-so-young girls all over the world were singing that song by heart. I knew it was a thing when the nine-year-old daughter of friends sang it for us at dinner one night. This is a very healthy young lady who—unlike her peers—doesn't really care what's happening on social media. Yet she knew it by heart, not something you can master in one viewing of the movie. I later saw a YouTube video of soldiers garrisoned in Afghanistan singing along. "Let It Go" is, safe to say, a phenomenon.

In the film, Elsa is the young snow queen of a mythic Nordic kingdom, a girl with a unique gift, perhaps curse. She has the Midas touch, except everything she embraces turns to ice. After years of isolation, during her public "coming out party," she accidentally sets off a series of catastrophic freezing and flees to the mountains both to save her people and to escape shame and scorn over what she has done. Enter the song that captured something in the social psyche. She sings that she will never let anyone in, she will rule a kingdom of isolation, and she doesn't care. Let it go. She is finally carefree.

Of course, she's far from carefree: she's hurt and she *does* care; she's an adolescent girl running from pain. A wild horse in flight. The song really isn't so much about a healthy letting go as it is about willful denial. A more accurate title would have been "I Will Shut My Heart Down." It's not release; it's fortressing. Literally. The climax of her song has Elsa finishing the creation of her ice castle. Alone.

This is not what benevolent detachment looks like. Elsa's letting go is angry and defiant. But it sure touched something in the cultural imagination. As did the 2018 book *The Subtle Art of Not Giving a F*ck*. Pardon the language, but it caught my attention because this little paperback by a relatively unknown author has sold *millions* of copies. The author touched upon an ache within us. He actually isn't cynical; he makes the important case that you simply cannot care about everything all the time. Which I think tells us that millions of people are feeling massively overburdened and looking for some way to lighten their heavy emotional load.

This is something Jesus is particularly good at helping us with, which is why learning benevolent detachment is such a timely grace.

GIVE EVERYONE AND EVERYTHING TO ME

I got home from work on a Friday afternoon a few weeks ago and went outside to just sit, be quiet, try to find God. Nothing big. No crisis. Not a seven-day fast. Just sitting quietly, attempting to dial back into his presence. It was astounding how many things presented themselves in a matter of about five minutes. Things I forgot to do at work. Emails I still needed to send. Emails I needed to now send to correct emails I shouldn't have sent. The One Minute Pause is where I began. It created the space for me to then practice benevolent detachment—my only rescue.

You can't sort all this stuff out.

And you sure can't wait to find God and life and restoration until you've sorted your life out. There's too much rushing at us; we haven't the time to carefully and systematically think through every piece of information, misspoken word, confusing interaction, heartbreaking news. Subtly, maybe not so subtly, the burdens on the soul pile up.

I have a friend who is one of those beautiful people with the gift of seeing the spiritual world while they walk around in the physical world. One of his particular giftings is that he sees people's "backpacks." "Everyone has a backpack," he says. He is referring to their burdens; he sees their burdens as backpacks they carry around with them. "Some people's backpacks are bigger than others," he says. "They're filled with past regrets, present concerns, and fears about their future. But some are wonderfully small and light. Everyone has one."

Worry is only one of a hundred things that burden our souls. Genuine concern is just as dangerous, maybe more so because it's grounded in something noble—your concerns for your aging parents, a sick friend, a people group, a cause crying out for justice. A friend of mine runs a home rescuing trafficked girls. He wrote last week to say that the government facility is overcrowded, and they asked him if he could take eleven girls. The heartbreak was my friend had room for only five; he had to make the brutal call. Today a therapist colleague who does remarkable work with military men and women suffering PTSD lamented he can't see enough people. "We're losing too many to suicide," he said. "It tears me up I can't help more."

Those kinds of things can fill a backpack and make it mighty heavy.

Jesus began teaching me about benevolent detachment almost two years ago. Every time I would turn to him with a question, he would say, *Give everyone and everything to me.* The invitation rang so true; I knew I needed to learn this. So I began to practice it as best I could. But then Jesus kept repeating the invitation. I'd be asking about something entirely unrelated to the people in my life—car repairs, scheduling a trip, my tax returns—and Jesus would reply, *Give everyone and everything to me.* It was irritating. I finally realized that the reason he kept repeating it was because I wasn't practicing it very well. I was carrying people. Worrying about things.

We are far more entangled with the world than we know. And the thing is, people and causes have a way of entangling themselves with *you* too.

Some of this has to do with the moment we live in and the obliteration of social boundaries.

Thanks to social media, everyone's life is open and accessible through Facebook, Twitter, Instagram—all of it. We've created an assumption that you can enter and observe, or engage, with anyone, anywhere, anytime. There are no boundaries. We've created an assumption that we're entitled to enter anyone else's private space at any time. It's very harmful. Cell phones have been a major contributor to this loss of personal space. A friend who is a successful businessman explained to me how the rules of corporate loyalty have changed: "They expect you to be available anytime, day or night, because of this," he said, holding up his phone. "They can text you, call you 24/7. You are now considered to be available anytime, all the time. Those are the new rules."

I told myself as I drove off into the wilderness this morning that I would turn my phone off for a few days to enforce my disengagement. But I've checked my messages several times in the last hour. It's so odd to be dialed into the technology of the world while I drive through rural countryside. This was the world of my grandmother, raised her entire life in rural America. Back in the day if you wanted to have a conversation with someone, if you wanted to enter their world, you literally had to enter their world. You got in your car and drove to their farm and sat on their porch and had a conversation. You also understood that there are appropriate hours for doing so. People were very aware that there were public moments and private moments, public spaces and private spaces.

All that is completely gone now.

People have this unspoken assumption they can enter your world anytime. It's suffocating to the soul; there's no breathing room. No wonder books like *Boundaries* and *The Subtle Art of Not Giving a F*ck* are selling millions. People are looking for some way to push this stuff back just a few feet. Gimme some space for heaven's sake.

Exactly.

Benevolent detachment is your way out.

GIVING IT A TRY

I know, I know—you've got all sorts of pushback going on inside even as you read this. "This sounds impossible; you don't know my world." "But what about loving? What about caring?" "How is it right to just let things go?"

Quite simply, because you're not God.

You can't save the world. You can't even carry it.

23

"Who of you by worrying can add a single hour to your life? Since you cannot do this very little thing, why do you worry about the rest?" (Luke 12:25–26). Jesus is quite serious about turning everything over to him, actually. So let's repeat the invitation:

Are you tired? Worn out? Burned out on religion? Come to me. Get away with me and you'll recover your life. I'll show you how to take a real rest. Walk with me and work with me—watch how I do it. Learn the unforced rhythms of grace. I won't lay anything heavy or ill-fitting on you. Keep company with me and you'll learn to live freely and lightly. (Matthew 11:28–30 THE MESSAGE)

Cast all your anxiety on him because he cares for you. (1 Peter 5:7) Live carefree before God; he is most careful with you. (THE MESSAGE)

These aren't suggestions. The Bible is not a book of suggestions. You've got to release the world; you've got to release people, crises, trauma, intrigue, all of it. There has to be sometime in your day where you just let it all go. All the tragedy of the world, the heartbreak, the latest shooting, earthquake—the soul was *never* meant to endure this. The soul was never meant to inhabit a world like this. It's way too much. Your soul is finite. You cannot carry the sorrows of the world. Only God can do that. Only he is infinite. Somewhere, sometime in your day, you've just got to release it. You've got to let it go.

We need to make this clear—the invitation of God is an

unburdened life. Come, you who are heavy laden. Cast your cares upon him. Live carefree before God. It's practically a party invitation. One of the least understood disciplines of the spiritual life. And therefore a wonderful place of discovery for each of us, and a truly liberating opportunity to experience more of God in our everyday experience.

Benevolent detachment takes practice. The One Minute Pause is a good place to start. "I give everyone and everything to you, God. I give everyone and everything to you." Often I find I need to follow that up with some specifics: "I give my children to you," for I worry about them. "I give that meeting to you." "I give this book to you." As you do this, pay attention—your soul will tell you whether or not you're releasing. If the moment after you pray you find yourself mulling over the very thing you just released, you haven't released it. Go back and repeat the process until it feels that you have.

Bedtime is ideal; Stasi and I now do it every night. "Jesus, we give everyone and everything to you." And then we usually have to name some things. "We give you our kids. We give you our aging mother. We give you what blew up at work today. We give you our ministry and mission in the world, which we care so much about—all those hurting people. We give you the Florida shooting. We can't carry this, God. We release it all to you."

As you practice release, what you're doing is creating soul space; you are literally carving out the intellectual and emotional space for God to come in.

If you build it, he will come. He *wants* to fill you.

By the way, benevolent detachment is a gift to the people in your life. Far too often we saddle people with our expectations, hopes, and needs too. Most of the time subconsciously, but we do it nevertheless. With our need to be seen. To be celebrated. To be understood. You actually do people an enormous favor when you practice benevolent detachment, because *they'd* like to be disentangled from *you* too.

You get to break free, dear ones, "like a horse in open country" (Isaiah 63:13).

three

DRINKING BEAUTY

Summer wildflowers are one of the reasons I'm so grateful to live in Colorado. I grew up in the strip-mall suburbs of Los Angeles; if we wanted to see wildflowers, we had to drive an hour out of town, up the Cajon Pass or out east to the desert. But here in the Rocky Mountain West—for a few wonderful months each summer—we have wildflowers galore. Blues of every shade; reds running from orange through crimson to pink; yellows and whites, like the palette of a good watercolor set.

One of my favorites is a lovely little fellow so easy to miss—the Many Flowered Aster, a collection of quaint little daisy-like blossoms about the size of a dime. In summer they grow profusely in clusters five inches above the ground, bright little white petals with yellow centers. Come fall they dry to a straw color standing where they were, looking like tiny little wicker baskets. Last night there was a freezing rain, and each little basket is now covered in a delicate ice.

It makes them look like miniature crystal goblets, hundreds of them, as if the field mice were preparing a banquet.

Human beings need oxygen in order to live. Lots of it. So our loving God provided us a world completely engulfed in oxygen; we swim in life-giving air like fish swim in water. Put your arm out—it's surrounded with oxygen. Look down at your feet—they're wading through it too. God also arranged for the daily replenishment of this planet-wide ocean of oxygen, through the forest and jungles and even the algae of the seas. We take it in all day long, and all day long he renews it. Lavish. And a good thing too!

He's done the same with water. We need it daily. No human being can go without it for more than four days. Our planet is called the "blue planet" because of the amount of water we have. The oceans, of course, and the rain cycle that draws water from them and spreads it over the earth. Streams, ponds, rivers, lakes— the generosity of God can be seen here too. Without water nothing lives. Think of what happens to your lovely flowers when they are deprived of water.

Now, with the same generosity and care, God also filled the world with a renewable supply of something our souls need daily: beauty. Yes, beauty. The fact that our world is so saturated with beauty, breathtaking in so many ways great and small—this ought to let you know God feels it's something you need for your survival. We are absolutely swimming in it.

But apart from the artist and poet, most people don't intentionally pursue beauty as nourishment. Notice that beauty doesn't make the typical lists of discipleship models, spiritual disciplines, or soul care. Even in his wonderful, seminal book on healing trauma—*The Body Keeps the Score*—Dr. Bessel van der Kolk barely refers to it. That baffles me. Beauty is one of the richest graces God has provided to heal our souls and absorb his goodness.

BEAUTY'S POWER

My trek through Wyoming and Montana took me to Yellowstone, one of my favorite places on earth. No, I don't like the crowds. But there's a simple secret to Yellowstone—if you're willing to get half a mile off the pavement, you can have one of the largest contiguous wildernesses practically to yourself. I did brave the crowds, though, to see the falls of the Yellowstone River as it plunges into the Grand Canyon of the Yellowstone. Thomas Moran did a gorgeous painting of it after he came through with the Hayden expedition in 1871; his artwork was one of the things that helped convince Congress to make this the first of our national parks.

Artist's Point looks back up at the falls from a half mile down canyon. It is breathtaking; of course painters love its panorama. But it was overcrowded, so I went on my way to find some space of my own in the woods for the day. Later that evening, driving back to my campsite before dark, I passed a sign on the north side of the falls that read "Brink of Falls." I'd never taken this route before. The trail has a stern warning at the top, that you're about to plunge six hundred feet down and you'd better be prepared to make the climb back. Knowing this would sift out most tourists and curious what the brink was like, I descended. You can walk right to the edge and look down, where thousands of cubic feet of water plunge each second over the precipice, dropping more than twice the height of Niagara Falls into the exploding spray and clouds of mist boiling back up from far below.

It's hard to describe the experience. The river is clear, smooth, translucent green right as it slips over the brink. Looking down it becomes a churning cataract of unceasing, foaming waves plunging into the abyss, like the breakers of ocean waves but one on top of another, all spray and foam and deep hues, green in the depths at the top, turning lavender in the long plunge. Water is so life-giving, and the deluging cataract was not violent, but forceful in its plentitude. Living majesty, unceasingly renewed. So as I leaned over, all I saw was the foaming deluge pouring down, down, down in white billows through which jade greens, soft blues, and lavender appeared and disappeared, pouring down with such grace I practically went with it. I later told Stasi, "It looked like the glory of God; if it had been, I would have thrown myself in."

I stood there watching the surging, pulsating, thundering beauty for I don't know how long, unmoving, as people came and went. I was more than transfixed; I was held in the grip of beauty so abundant, so glorious and alive I could feel it healing my soul. You see, I had taken this trip largely because I, too, felt traumatized. I'd been through too much death to recount here, and it seemed my entire journey was divinely orchestrated to bring me to this place.

Beauty comforts. Beauty heals. Why else would we send flowers to a hospital room or funeral?

I've been personally convinced of this for years, so it was with delight I opened a lovely little book a friend recommended: *On Beauty and Being Just* by Harvard aesthetics professor Elaine Scarry. The author is trying to restore the high place of beauty in a skeptical world:

> Beauty is life-saving. . . . Augustine described it as "a plank amid the waves of the sea." Proust makes a version of this claim over and over again. Beauty quickens. It adrenalizes. It makes the heart beat faster. It makes life more vivid, animated, living, worth living. . . . It is as though one has suddenly been washed up onto a merciful beach.[1]

That's it—beauty rescues. It rescues because it is merciful, comforting. It heals, restores, revives, renews. This is why people in convalescence want to sit in a garden, or by a window overlooking the sea. Research shows that patients recovered faster, needed fewer pain killers, and left the hospital sooner if their windows allowed views of nature.[2] "The pleasure we take in beauty is inexhaustible," writes Scarry. "No matter how long beautiful things endure, they cannot out-endure our longing for them."[3]

Stasi and I were on a mission of sorts to the UK last spring, a whirlwind trip with something like nineteen engagements in nine days. We spent two nights in the London suburb of St. Albans, one of those trendy little British towns where cobblestones streets and fifteenth-century buildings meet art galleries and upscale restaurants. It was crowded, unusually hot, with lots and *lots* of traffic. My sensitivity was probably heightened by my exhaustion—and the exhaust—but the sound of motorcycles roaring up and down the narrow streets was really getting on my nerves. What was charming soon felt harming. At that moment I received a text from my wife, who had left the thoroughfare earlier to go in search of the cathedral: "Come to the cathedral; step inside."

As soon as I entered the garden-like grounds I began to feel better. Grass. Flowers. Trees. I stepped into the sanctuary and found myself alone. Coolness. Soft, colored light filtered down through the stained glass windows. The heavy stone structure held out every bit of city noise. Far up in front, hidden from view, the chapel choir was practicing. It was heavenly, and thus it was healing. Heaven always heals. Beauty heals, partly because it *proclaims* that there is goodness in the world and that goodness prevails, or is preserved, or will somehow outlast all harm and darkness.

"The moment of perceiving something beautiful confers on the perceiver the gift of life."[4]

Beauty also sings to us songs of abundance.

Two days before the falls of Yellowstone, I spent an afternoon seated in a camp chair high above a lake in the Wind River Mountains, simply drinking in the valley before me. The lake and granite cliffs were like Yosemite, gorgeous and grand, but my eyes were continually drawn to the evergreen forests on the mountain slopes. These are well-watered forests, so thick and lush it seemed I could see a million trees along a few miles of slope. My soul loved it, and I tried to pay attention to why. It had to do with abundance. One tree is a miracle; a hundred trees a celebration. But the staggering presence of tens of thousands of tall, thriving evergreens in dense profusion fills the soul with memories of Eden, visions that speak messages. "Beautiful things, as Matisse shows, always carry greetings from other worlds within them."[5] The Christian understands those greetings to come from the kingdom of God itself.

But most of all, beauty *reassures*. This is especially important to our search here for the grace beauty offers our life with God. We need reassuring.

Beauty reassures us that goodness is still real in the world, more real than harm or scarcity or evil. Beauty reassures us of abundance, especially that God is absolutely abundant in goodness and in life. Beauty reassures us there is plenty of life to be had. I believe beauty reassures us that the end of this Story is wonderful. The French impressionist Matisse "repeatedly said that he wanted to make paintings so serenely beautiful that when one came upon them, suddenly all problems would subside."[6]

Beauty is such a gentle grace. Like God, it rarely shouts, rarely intrudes. Rather it woos, soothes, invites; it romances and caresses. We often sigh in the presence of beauty as it begins to minister to us—a good, deep soul-sigh.

GIVING IT A TRY

You don't need to travel far to find beauty. God has strewn it around the globe in such generous portions we have only to stop and notice, paying particular attention to the intimate. Yes, epic beauty is worth traveling to see—the Himalayas, the Maasai Mara, Yosemite, any tropic island. But intimate beauty is just as healing, perhaps more so, and available everywhere. (I shared the St. Albans story to remind my urban readers beauty can be found even in noisy, congested cities.)

It snowed yesterday, just a few inches. Last night strong winds followed. When I first stepped out for a morning walk, all I was aware of was that I was cold and didn't want to go. But I needed the walk, so I pressed into it. Cold makes you hunker down, cinch up your jacket, and burrow into your hood. It makes your body and soul brace against the world, keeps you from participating in the barefoot openness that summer does so well. I was trudging along the sidewalk head down, trying to keep the wind out of my jacket, when it happened. My focus was only on the few feet of ground in front of me when suddenly beauty broke forth in the patterns of the crusted snow. Multitudes of tiny windswept dunes, two or three inches high, looking like a satellite view of the desert. Wave after wave of little undulating ridges in curvilinear symmetry, like a sea frozen in time. My world was reduced—or expanded—to a few square feet of frozen front yard, like an aerial view of the Sahara in all its elegant barrenness and vast empty beauty.

Really—beauty is all around us. In the shimmering shadows

sunlight creates through any foliage. The intricate pattern and color of tree bark (stop and look; touch it). The way sunlight falls on your kitchen table in the morning. The grain of wood. Songbirds in your neighborhood. Fabric. Candlelight. The infinitely creative patterns of frost. The frost on the stalks of dried grasses this morning looked like tiny gladiolas made of glass or the calligraphy of fairies. Water in almost any form. Water on a blade of grass. Water drops on leaves. Leaves themselves—their shape, texture, the lacelike patterns running through them. A field of grass, especially as the wind plays through it. Fields of corn, wheat, any crop. The stars, the moon in all its phases. Rain-washed streets in the city at night, drops of water on your windshield. Human faces are infinitely beautiful. And I have not even mentioned flowers, vases, music, fine art, and the beautiful things we use to decorate our homes.

Given beauty's healing effects, given how it soothes the soul and opens us up to the goodness of God, I hope you will intentionally do two things:

Receive it for the gift it is! Pause, and let the beauty minister to you. *I receive this into my soul.* Too often we just notice and go on, like a pedestrian who steps over a hundred-dollar bill lying on the sidewalk. Stop and pick it up! In these moments you open yourself and receive the beauty, the gift, the grace—receive it into your being. Let it bring to you God's love, his tenderness, his rich goodness. We live so braced, not openly, but quite subtly—braced for the day, braced by the assault on our attention, braced by the noise around us.

Pause when you are offered beauty and make the conscious

decision, *I receive this grace.* We open our clenched soul to let it in. To find God in it. I will often pray, *Thank you for this beauty. I receive it into my soul. And with it I receive you, in it, by it, through it—your love, your goodness, your life.*

That receiving part is key.

Sometimes I use the One Minute Pause simply to drink in some small beauty before me. And sigh.

Second, fill your world with beauty, as Harvard professor Scarry realized she had to do one especially bleak winter:

> My house, though austere inside, is full of windows banking onto a garden. The garden throws changing colors into the chaste rooms—lavenders, pinks, blues, and pools of green. One winter when I was bereft because my garden was underground, I put Matisse prints all over the walls—thirteen in a single room.[7]

Thirteen impressionist prints in one room. There you go. Fill your life with beauty or reminders of it. When we are harried, haunted, in fight or flight, beauty seems a luxury for people on vacation. Just the opposite is true—it's a lifeline being thrown to you from heaven.

four

SIMPLE UNPLUGGING

I'm sitting at my desk this morning, writing. My phone, lying face-down next to me, vibrates. Because yes, I did silence it, but I didn't turn it off. The vibration notification causes a reflex response in me, a learned response. I pick it up, read the text that just came in, reply, set it down, and turn back to my work. But it takes me a few moments to recover my train of thought. Meanwhile, I remember that a friend sent me a link to an article that applies to what I'm writing this morning, so I decide to have a look now that I'm no longer engaged in the actual act of writing. The article is helpful and does get my thoughts rolling again, but as you know, when you get to any news website you don't simply receive the article. You're confronted with a visual experience that is one third article and two thirds advertising—and which of those is typically more arresting?

I get five seconds into the article when a pop-up screen requests my email address.

This stuff is so irritating.

I switch screens (for, of course, I have multiple screens open in the background, as most desktop and mobile users do) to one of those helpful online Bible programs so I can look up a verse. Quicker than I can type "Psalm 1," Google ads pop up in banners and columns on the right and left side of the screen. Google knows my buying habits—Google actually knows a freaky amount of information about me and you—and suddenly here are all sorts of ads perfectly tailored to get my attention. The hunting pack I was looking at for my son's birthday, the exact earrings I bought my wife and four others like them. There are videos and moving banners, and they are *so* distracting.

I realize now I'm totally removed from writing, so I choose to settle back into the presence of Christ with some worship. I was listening to something on YouTube earlier, so that screen is open in the background too. But of course the worship does not play first; first comes the movie trailer, car promotion, something marketing geniuses spent millions on because they know they have five seconds before I get to click Skip Ad.

Finally, like a man who has run the gauntlet, I am able to return to my work. Then another notification on my phone: my weather app is alerting me of possible snow flurries this evening, and while I pick it up to turn the thing off entirely, a video pops up of some bizarre sea creature washed up on the beaches of Florida, "never before seen by man!"

This is our daily. This is the stuff that comes at us all the time.

It's like driving at night into a snowstorm, your headlights illuminating the flurries racing at your windshield. It's all you can see. No wonder so few people enjoy the graces of beauty or practice benevolent detachment. Or even find it possible to take a moment's pause. Our attention is constantly being taken hostage.

THE ASSAULT ON YOUR ATTENTION

Now that we're getting a handle on just how damaging technology is, particularly hours of screen time, there is a robust discussion on what responsible use of technology looks like. Particularly for minors. (Succumbing to pressure, Apple made their screen time report built into the iPhone.) For heaven's sake—now that we know social media use is correlated to increased depression and anxiety, do we really need further evidence to convince us to limit our use of it?[1] I share those concerns and keep my personal screen time to a bare minimum. But it was only when I opened Matthew Crawford's excellent book *The World Beyond Your Head* that I saw the bigger picture—the insistent, unrelenting assault on our *attention*.

News. Marketing. Notifications. Alerts. Status updates. Postings. An incessant barrage of "information" competing for our attention. You can't get away from it. I fly a bit for my living, and airlines know you are a captive audience. Before takeoff, but once I'm buckled in my seat, ads begin to play on the screen before me, and I can't turn them off. Walk through a modern airport—it's a shopping mall designed like a casino, hard to find your way out. I leave the airport and jump in a cab; a screen facing me immediately starts playing commercials, loudly. Driving down the highway my attention is arrested by electronic billboards. All of this stimuli demands our attention:

> The introduction of novelty into one's field of view commands what the cognitive psychologists call an orienting response (an important evolutionary adaptation in a world of predators): an animal turns its face and eyes toward the new thing. A new thing typically appears every second on television. The images on the screen jump out of the flow of experience and make a demand on us.[2]

The harm here is not simply in the numbing effects of technology. As I mentioned in the introduction, Americans consume something like 10 hours of media a day,[3] over 100,000 words and 34 gigabytes—which would crash a laptop in a week.[4] What does the constant barrage of the trivial, urgent, mediocre, traumatic, heartbreaking, or buffoonish do to us when it comes in an unending stream—unfiltered, unexplained, unproven, unexpected, most of it unworthy—yet nevertheless we pay attention on demand?

Then I read the book I mentioned earlier, *The Shallows: What the Internet Is Doing to Our Brains*, for which Nicholas Carr nearly won the Pulitzer Prize. He begins by recounting numerous conversations with very bright men and women, PhDs in their fields, who all confessed a similar phenomenon: the noticeable deterioration of their attention.

Even though these intellectuals live and move in the world of books, research, literature, Carr was startled to corroborate so many reports that they couldn't read books anymore. Couldn't read articles, hadn't the patience even for a long blog post.[5] He goes on to document how the Internet is reshaping not only our ability to take in information, it is altering the structures of our brains. We don't like being asked to focus on anything for very long anymore; we are adapted to the quick, short stimulus of the internet and our mobile devices.[6]

I think you know the zip, zip, zip effect all this is having on your attention. Part of what makes this troubling, Carr notes, is this:

> It's not only deep thinking that requires a calm, attentive mind. It's also empathy and compassion. Psychologists have long studied how people experience fear and react to threats, but it's only recently that they've begun researching the sources of our nobler instincts. What they're finding is that, as Antonio Damasio, the director of USC's Brain and Creativity Institute, explains, the higher emotions emerge from neural processes that "are inherently slow. . . ."
>
> The writer of a cover story in *New York* magazine says that as we become used to the "21st-century task" of "flitting" among bits of online information, "the wiring of the brain will inevitably change . . ." We may lose our capacity "to concentrate on a complex task from beginning to end," but in recompense we'll gain new skills, such as the ability to "conduct 34 conversations simultaneously across six different media."

Carr's conclusion is worth repeating here:

The "frenziedness of technology," Heidegger wrote, threatens to "entrench itself everywhere." It may be that we are now entering the final stage of that entrenchment. We are welcoming the frenziedness into our souls.[7]

You already knew this from your own experience; your frenzied soul has been trying to tell you for some time.

But we frogs don't yet see the real implications of this warming kettle.

Down through the ages, followers of Christ have believed that to be able to give God our attention as a regular practice was a *very* important thing. After vividly recounting the many challenges of faith and character before us, the author of Hebrews says,

Let us run with endurance the race God has set before us. We do this by keeping [fixing] our eyes on Jesus, the champion who initiates and perfects our faith (Hebrews 12:1–2 NLT).

Those who look to him are radiant (Psalm 34:5)

Oh, how I love your law!
I meditate on it all day long.
Your commands are always with me
and make me wiser than my enemies.

I have more insight than all my teachers,

for I meditate on your statutes. (Psalm 119:97–99)

I don't think we realize how much our use of technology and its assault on our attention has made this difficult to do. You can't give God your attention when your attention is constantly being targeted and taken captive . . . and you're cooperating.

In a blog post entitled "Mobile Blindness," marketing guru Seth Godin writes,

> We swipe instead of click, we scan instead of read, even our personal email. We get exposure to far more at the surface, but we rarely dig in. As a result, the fine print gets ignored. We go for headlines, not nuance. It's a deluge of gossip and thin promises . . . blog posts and tweets are getting shorter. We rarely stick around for the long version. "Photo-keratitis," "snow blindness," happens when there's too much ultraviolet, when the fuel for our eyes comes in too strong and we can't absorb it. Something similar is happening to each of us, to our entire culture as a result of the tsunami of noise vying for our attention.[8]

Mobile blindness. The quick pass. The inability to linger and dig deep. It's just the next thing, the next thing, the next thing. Our precious attention has been groomed and taken hostage. Let's contrast that with Psalm 1 (the verse I extracted out of my own assaultive experience earlier today):

Blessed is the one

who does not walk in step with the wicked,

or stand in the way that sinners take

or sit in the company of mockers,

but whose delight is in the law of the LORD,

and who meditates on his law day and night.

That person is like a tree planted by streams of water,

which yields its fruit in season,

and whose leaf does not wither—

whatever they do prospers.

Not so the wicked!

They are like chaff

that the wind blows away. (Psalm 1:1–4)

Two types of people are being contrasted here, two types of experience: The first type is rooted and substantive and so life giving. Then there is the person so lacking in substance, so ephemeral that their reality is compared to dandelion puffs, chaff, that a breath of wind can sweep away. The key is this: the rooted person is able to meditate—*give sustained attention to*—the revelation of God. Not swipe, not multitask. Lingering focus. So Crawford wonders, "As our mental lives become more fragmented, what is at stake often seems to be nothing less than the question of whether one can maintain a coherent self. I mean a self that is able to act according to settled purposes and ongoing projects, rather than flitting about."[9]

Dear reader—you can't find more of God when all you're able to give him is a flit and flicker of your attention.

IN LOVE WITH DISTRACTION

Stasi and I celebrated our thirty-fifth wedding anniversary with a trip to Kauai. We find it the most gorgeous of the Hawaiian Islands, maybe one of the most beautiful places on earth. Volcanic cliffs covered with lush tropical forest spill right down to the water's edge. Hibiscus blossoms fall onto the peaceful rivers that wind their way through the jungle. This isn't your tourist Hawaii. Apart from Princeville, the North Shore is way laid back, and after you cross a couple one-lane bridges, you feel you really could be on the outskirts of Eden.

Sitting on a quiet beach there, with no one to our right or left for more than two hundred yards of pristine white sand, it was so luscious I expected Adam and Eve to go strolling by any moment. Now, you'd think this would be enough to delight, enchant, and soothe any soul, but as I took a stroll down the beach myself, I passed a guy sitting under a banyan tree—watching videos on his iPhone.

Wow.

You can't unplug from your technology even in paradise?

Now, to be fair, I bet this is what happened: He had his phone with him—because everybody always has their phone with them—and somebody texted him a funny YouTube video, and he couldn't resist the urge, and that was that. He was glued to a little artificial screen watching some cat sit on a toilet, when all around him was beauty beyond description, the very beauty his soul needed, and filling that beauty and coming through it the presence of God.

And I saw myself in this guy.

Because I, too, had brought my phone with me to the beach, and I, too, responded when the little "chirp" alerted me to an incoming text. (We always have our excuses; every addict does. I was "keeping myself available to my children.") Every notification got my attention, because it triggered the brain's learned response to check out what news had just come in.

> Dopamine causes you to want, desire, seek out, and search. . . . It is the opioid system (separate from dopamine) that makes us feel pleasure. . . . The wanting system propels you to action and the liking system makes you feel satisfied and therefore pause your seeking. If your seeking isn't turned off at least for a little while, then you start to run in an endless loop [Dopamine Loop]. The dopamine system is stronger than the opioid system. You tend to seek more than you are satisfied. . . . Dopamine starts you seeking, then you get rewarded for the seeking which makes you seek more. It becomes harder and harder to stop looking at email, stop texting, or stop checking your cell phone to see if you have a message or a new text. . . . The dopamine system doesn't have satiety built in. It is possible for the dopamine system to keep saying "more more more," causing you to keep seeking even when you have found the information.[10]

Neo was never so totally and completely trapped in the Matrix.

Since denial is one of the stages of addiction, let me ask you, dear reader, a couple questions: When your little Chime, Glass, or Swoosh sound alerts you to an incoming text, do you easily ignore it and go on with the conversation you are having, or reading what you are reading, or enjoying the back seat view as you drive through the desert? I'm serious—when that thing vibrates in your pocket, do you regularly ignore it? Or do you automatically reach to see? Can you shut your phone off when you get home in the evening and not turn it on again until morning? When you first wake, do you allow yourself a leisurely coffee and bagel before you look at your phone—or is your phone the very first thing you look at every morning?

Yeah, me too. Let's be honest: we *prefer* distraction. The more distracted we are, the less present we are to our souls' various hurts, needs, disappointments, boredom, and fears. It's a short-term relief with long-term consequences. What blows my mind is how totally normal this has become; it's the new socially acceptable addiction. I've got a friend who decided to break with his; he now turns his phone off over the weekend. I text him, and he doesn't reply until Sunday night or Monday morning. I'm embarrassed by my irritation: *C'mon, man—you know the protocol. Everybody agrees to be totally available, anywhere, anytime, 24/7. It's what we do.*

What does it say that you look like some sort of nut job when you turn your phone off?

The brother of Jesus was trying to offer some very simple guidelines to a true life with God when, among other things, he said,

"Religion that God our Father accepts as pure and faultless is this: to look after orphans and widows in their distress and to keep oneself from being polluted by the world" (James 1:27). That unpolluted part—that's what worries me, when the average American checks their phone eighty times a day (!), and 70 percent said they sleep with their phone within reach.[11]

BUT WE HAVE A CHOICE

Finding more of God, growing strong in soul and spirit, requires creating space in your day for God—to intentionally put yourself in a place that allows you to draw upon and experience the healing power of the life of God filling you. Over the ages, serious followers of Jesus have used stillness and quiet, worship, fasting, prayer, beautiful places, and a number of other "exercises" to drink deeply of the presence of God. And untangle their souls from the world.

The ongoing deluge of intriguing facts and commentary, scandal and crisis, genuinely important guidance combined with the latest insider news from around the globe, and our friends' personal lives gives the soul a medicated feeling of awareness, connection, and meaning. Really, it's the new Tower of Babel—the immediate access to every form of "knowledge" and "groundbreaking" information right there on our phones, every waking moment. It confuses the soul into a state of artificial meaning and purpose, all the while preventing genuine soul care and life with God. Who has time to read a book? Plant a garden?

Let me say it again, because it's so counter to the social air we breathe: what has become the normal daily consumption of input is numbing the soul with artificial meaning and purpose while in fact the soul grows thinner and thinner through neglect, harmed by the very madness that passes for a progressive life. We are literally being forced into the "shallows" of our life.

I'm not scolding; I'm tossing a lifeline.

Sincere followers of Jesus in every age have faced very difficult decisions—usually at that point of tension where their life with and for God ran straight against the prevailing cultural norm. The new Tower of Babel is ours. We have always been "strangers and aliens" in the world, insofar as our values seemed so strange and bizarre to those around us. We are now faced with a series of decisions that are going to make us look like freaks—choices like fasting from social media, never bringing our smartphones to any meal, conversation, or Bible study, cutting off our media intake so we can practice stillness every day.

The good news is that we actually have a choice. Unlike persecution, the things currently assaulting us are things we can choose not to participate in.

GIVING IT A TRY

And you're already doing it—you're reading a book! Well done!

As we go along, you'll discover many wonderful ways to unplug and be whole. For now, a few thoughts on technology . . .

- **Turn off notifications.** You don't need to know when your aunt posted another picture of her dog on Facebook; you can check when you have set aside time to do so. You don't need to know about the snowstorm in Ohio or the embarrassing thing the president just said.
- **Fast from social media.** Try cutting your use by 50 percent for one week and see what it does for you. (Many of our friends loved it so much they've decided to pretty much get off social media altogether.)
- **Turn your phone off at 8:00 p.m.** Give yourself some evening time for real things. And banish all technology from your bedroom.
- **Don't check your phone as soon as you wake up in the morning.** Give your soul mercy to wake up; enjoy a few peaceful moments.
- **When your phone chirps or vibrates, don't react.** Make it wait till you pick it up. In these small ways I'm making my phone a tool again, something that serves me instead of the other way around.
- **Do real things.** Chop vegetables, play cards, do a puzzle, go for a walk, learn an instrument.

If you create a little bit of sacred space every day, God will meet you there. And you will begin to love it.

five

KINDNESS TOWARD OURSELVES

Our beloved family dog is dying. But I'm not going to drag you through that tragedy; I want to share something gracious I'm learning through it.

Only yesterday our vet told us that our sweet Golden Retriever is very ill, and tonight we're supposed to go out to dinner with some friends. I'm torn, because we've been scheduling, canceling, and rescheduling this dinner for six months, and part of me really wants to go. But part of me is dealing with the loss of the family dog. What I'm aware of in this moment is how often I need to put my soul aside in order to carry on with the demands of life. We all do. Life goes on, despite our personal struggles. You lose your father on a Wednesday; corporate America expects you back at the office Monday. It's hard on the soul. It's hard on our life with God.

But tonight I don't need to put my soul aside. Our friends are understanding; we can reschedule. The question is, why is practicing kindness toward my own soul so unfamiliar that it would be easy to ignore something as precious as the death of our dog to "carry on with things?" This world requires us to keep going at such speeds that we end up having only one emotional state toward everything—a general, haggard, hazy condition of "on." I'm on for this meeting; I'm on for this call with my mom; I'm on for the news the vet has. There's no margin for anything else.

> So we praise God for the glorious grace he has poured out on us who belong to his dear Son. He is so rich in kindness and grace that he purchased our freedom with the blood of his Son and forgave our sins. He has showered his kindness on us, along with all wisdom and understanding. (Ephesians 1:6–8 NLT)

God is rich in kindness, and he has showered kindness on us. This is so lovely and life-giving, we need to pause and reflect on it. Kindness. Such a simple virtue, it often takes a back seat to more dramatic qualities like bravery, holiness, or love (kindness sort of feels like the younger stepchild to love). And yet kindness is such a wonderful thing to receive.

Don't you love it when people are kind to you?

I sure do. In a world growing increasingly angry and hostile, a little bit of kindness can make your day. You're trying to merge into busy traffic and, instead of cutting you off, the driver ahead pauses and waves you in. You're returning some item to the store and, after waiting your turn behind several customers, you get to the counter only to realize you forgot the receipt. "No worries," the clerk says. "We can take care of this." Such simple gestures can totally change your day. Or how about this one—you're hurrying to get home because you promised some friends you'd watch their kids so they could get a rare date night, and you get pulled over for speeding. The officer hears your story and says, "I understand. How about you take it slow the rest of the way," and doesn't give you the ticket she could have.

Kindness is simply wonderful.

Now, the place I want to take us in this reflection is actually even more overlooked than offering kindness to one another. I'm struck by the power of offering kindness toward ourselves.

A KIND INVITATION

I'm working on a deck project this week. Specifically, I'm installing some deck railing. We haven't had any for years, but now Stasi and I are grandparents (at this point, two little girls entering full-on toddlerhood and a new little grandson), and suddenly I realize we need deck railing so our little adventurers don't take a plunge.

Anyhow, I'm out there for hours this morning trying to get one particularly stubborn rail in place. It's not going well, and I'm getting frustrated. But I'm kind of a push-through-it guy, and even though the temperature on the deck could roast a chicken, I keep at it another hour. No success. Finally, I realize what's needed—I need to walk away. I need to let it go. I need to come in and cool off and have lunch. This is new for me. Even though I've spent thirty years as a counselor teaching other people how to be gracious to their souls, I've always been rather hard on my own. So I'm learning to practice simple kindness toward myself. The fruit of it is really good on my soul; the ripple effects are good on everyone else around me.

A friend was in town last week. I felt I ought to invite them to come over. But before I sent the text, I paused and asked Jesus. *Not a good call*, he said. *You're utterly exhausted.* And it's true—I was wiped out from a week of meetings, mission, and work, and I was about to spend my one and only evening off on further giving, had not Jesus intervened. His counsel didn't come as a command; it came in the gentle spirit of kindness. *Don't do that to yourself.*

The practices I'm recommending in this book are offered in a spirit of kindness. I think it's the only posture that will enable us to embrace them, *enjoy* them, and maintain them over time. Practicing the One Minute Pause is kind. Making room for beauty is kind. Unplugging from the constant barrage of media coming at us is kind. I do these things because they bring me life; they bring me more of God; they heal and strengthen my soul. Because the results are wonderful! Because I'd be a fool not to.

So what might practicing kindness toward yourself look like these days? Perhaps in the way you talk to yourself, especially when you blow it, mess something up, let a friend down. It might be in the pace you are currently demanding your soul keep up with. What about the spoken and unspoken expectations you live by, or in the to-do list you currently have for yourself?

ON BEHALF OF OTHERS

"Love your neighbor as yourself," Jesus taught (Mark 12:31), implying a direct link between one and the other. Loving our neighbor is clearly an essential to Christian faith; I think we all get that one. But the qualifier "as yourself" is lost on most people; it confounded me for years. It almost sounds too pop psychology, something you'd see on the cover of the magazines at the checkout stand, right next to the articles on "brain superfoods" and "how to talk to your pet." Yet Jesus is pretty matter-of-fact about the comparison: Treat people like you treat yourself. Which I think has one of his brilliant hidden exposés in it, because we quickly realize if we treated our neighbor the way we typically treat ourselves, we wouldn't be great neighbors. Jesus thus drives home healthy self-care as tied to loving others. If that still sounds like something from Oprah, and not the New Testament, consider this: love your neighbor as yourself is "a horrible command," C. S. Lewis pointed out, "if the self were simply to be hated."[1]

The difficult truth we don't want to admit is this: the way you treat your own heart is the way you'll end up treating everyone else's.

We squirm; we don't like that. We counter, "No—I'm much more patient with my daughter than I am with myself." That may be so . . . in the short term. But over time our little frustrations begin to show themselves, and children—who are especially perceptive to approval and disapproval—can pick up the signals. If you are a "neatnick," I guarantee that you show more natural delight when your child straightens up their room to your standards than when they do a less-than-perfect job. The neatness touches your own issues, and you respond accordingly, "Wow—look at your room! You did a great job!" The child learns, *Mom likes me more when I'm neat.*

Most of the time we are completely unaware of how we treat our own heart. Our "way" with ourselves is simply our norm, and we've been at it so long we don't notice, in the same way we don't notice how much we bite our nails or finish our spouse's sentences for them. The father who doesn't allow himself his own emotions communicates so much to his children by that practice alone, and he further reinforces the lesson when he is visibly awkward and uncomfortable with the emotions of his child. He tries to hurry them through a "comforting" process: "I'm sorry, sweetheart. You'll feel better tomorrow." Or, "How about we get some ice cream?" He is thereby trying to rush the child through their emotions to a place of resolution, teaching them to be as abrupt with their own heart as he is with his.

So the fact remains: the way you treat your heart is the way you'll end up treating everyone else's.

None of this is meant to be shaming—not one bit. It's immensely hopeful! For one thing, you've picked up this book and progressed this far—that means you're seeking more of God, and learning to care for your soul (the vessel he fills). This right here is self-kindness, and it will spill over into kindness for those around you. I mentioned in the introduction the image of a fountain, gently overflowing with the waters of life, the soul that is receiving God in unceasing graces. Rainer Maria Rilke has a beautiful image of that fountain then pouring over into other basins around it, which would be the lives around us receiving the goodness that we are overflowing with:

> Two basins, one above the other, from
> within an ancient rounded marble rand.
> And from the top one, waters softly come,
> spilling to waters under them that stand
> and wait and meet their whispers.[2]

God is gentle; kindness is gentle. It flows both into us and through us in gentle whispers.

UNSPOKEN, UNREALISTIC EXPECTATIONS

I received another one of those videos the other day. An email from a friend with a link and the enticing line, "You've got to see this!" And it was impressive, no question. A beautifully filmed video of a professional dirt bike racer who had taken up surfing and wanted to combine his extreme adventures. So he constructed a dirt bike he could actually ride at high speeds on the ocean. Really. The gorgeous project was filmed in Tahiti. The climax of the video is him actually catching and surfing a wave on a motorcycle. Impressive. Outrageous. In the battle for our attention, this one is an easy winner; it's arresting.

And completely unkind. Because the cumulative effect of this stuff sets up all sorts of unspoken, maybe even unconscious expectations within us.

I don't think we've given any thought of what it does to the soul to live in a culture where that kind of stuff is the daily fare. This shows up in my inbox all the time; I know you get them too. First it was base jumping (folks leaping off cliffs and tall buildings wearing a parachute or parasail). That became routine, so it elevated to jumping without parachutes, in "squirrel suits," flying through the air to safe landing zones. Now that's routine, so the video I got the other day was of two guys jumping off a mountain with no safe landing zone within miles, flying in squirrel suits through the air and making their "landing" into the door of an airplane. The incessant upgrade of everything. Always pushing the boundaries. Extreme this, extreme that.

It sets up an unspoken set of expectations in our hearts that, unless your life is YouTube-worthy, your life is stupid. It's boring. (Why else would anxiety and depression—and envy—rise in direct proportion to one's consumption of social media? Because we're comparing our lives to what's online.) Creeping in is the message that if your life is going to measure up and be wonderful, it has to be fantastic. Men used to get on bended knee to propose to their beloved; nowadays you're a loser unless you do it skydiving or kayaking over waterfalls.

This phenomenon is shaping Christianity, or Christian practices, and even more harmfully shaping our spiritual expectations. Modern worship bands not only need to be *extraordinarily* talented musicians, young, and beautiful, but their live events employ multimedia to keep your attention as well. Now church services compete with concert-level staging, lighting, special effects, and films. The terrible, unspoken assumption creeping in is this: if you're going to find God, if you're going to have more of God, it's going to come through some amazing experience, something totally wild and over the top. Or we think that once we have God, the proof will be an over-the-top life. Not true. So unhelpful, and immensely unkind. This expectation actually makes those deeper experiences of God seem inaccessible for most of us.

We *do* need more of God, much more. Little sips between long droughts will not sustain us. We need more of God in our bodies, our souls, our relationships, our work, everywhere in our lives. But when you live in a culture of the incessant upgrade of everything, the sensational, it gives the impression that if you're going to have a deeper, richer, amazing experience of God, it's going to have to come in some sensational way.

I have some wonderful news for you: Nope. Not even close.

Life is built on the dailies. Consider love, friendship, and marriage.

Love, friendship, and marriage are not built on skydiving together, trips to Paris, kayaking the Amazon. They're not. Perhaps once in your life you might do something like that, but the fantastic is not your daily. Love, friendship, and marriage are nurtured in the context of simple things like coffee together, hanging out, getting a burrito, holding hands, taking a walk, doing the dishes, reading to one another, or just reading different things while you're together in the same room. It's the little things that build a beautiful life.

I love adventure. I love the ocean. I love rock climbing, canoeing, mountaineering, and motorcycle riding. But here's the deal—if you want to go to Yosemite and fulfill a lifelong dream of being a big wall climber, your daily doesn't look dramatic at all; it looks like doing pull-ups at home. If you want to take a motorcycle adventure trip through Scotland, the daily looks like getting on your bike and riding around town. Just going out and getting used to it. Dodging the neighborhood dog that always runs in front of you and stopping when the old lady brakes without warning. You're making it second nature so that when you *do* go out, you can handle the big wall climbing, the remarkable trips.

This is how life with God works, dear friends.

I think God has amazing things for us, I really do. I've been part of some extraordinary experiences with God. I've had global adventures with him. But I don't *live* there. Getting there, just like getting to love or anything else that's wonderful in this life, is in the dailies. It's back here in the little things we do. That is how we practice kindness towards ourselves—in the dailies.

GIVING IT A TRY

So let's return to kindness for a moment; we pursue these practices in a spirit of *kindness*.

What does extending kindness toward yourself look like right now?

How do you talk to yourself? What is your "way" with yourself? Is it harsh? Unforgiving?

What about the expectations you currently have for getting things done? Is efficiency the emperor of your life?

Pace of life is a good barometer too. What's the pace you're currently demanding of yourself? Would you ask the same pace of someone you love? Ask Jesus, *What is the pace you want for me right now, Lord?* He might have some things he'd like to say to you about that. Not in the negative sense, but in lovely directions toward life.

It was another hot day (Colorado has been scorching this summer), and I was inside waiting till things cooled off to go tend to our horses. Jesus whispered, *You should go now.* "Now?" *Yes—now.* So I got up and went. I noticed cumulus clouds building overhead (I love those great summer clouds), and as soon as I got to the barn it began to rain. So I slipped under an overhang and spent the next thirty minutes simply watching the wind in the tall grasses and the rain falling across the valley. It was absolutely lovely and so restoring. Beauty is so healing. I would have missed it all had I not listened.

The rain let up, I tended to our horses, and Jesus said, *You should head back now.* I didn't want to go back, but I obeyed. As soon as I got back to the house, a real gully-washer let loose—rain like a biblical flood.

A simple story. Nothing dramatic. But a beautiful picture of how God really does want to lead us into rest, beauty, and restoration.

Kindness means not expecting perfection in these practices, not requiring yourself to feel anything, being gracious about your heart's slow journey toward God.

SIX

ALLOWING FOR TRANSITIONS

One of my favorite books is *Horn of the Hunter,* the story of an African safari taken after World War II, written by the brilliant sportswriter Robert Ruark. I love the book because of the narrative of several months spent roaming the African wild when it was still largely wild. There is something romantic about the era of canvas tents and Land Rovers in a trackless African bush, with all the classic animals close by. On further reflection, I think I love the book because of the pace of life that is being recounted there. No one is in a hurry, neither man nor beast. There is a languid, almost sleepy rhythm to the saga, which fits the languid days and humid nights of the African savannah.

Back in Ruark's day, a trip to "Tanganyika" was truly an adventure to the ends of the earth. In the late '40s one flew by prop plane, slowly, from New York to London, London to Paris, Paris to Rome, Rome to Cairo, Cairo to Asmara, Asmara to Addis Ababa, Addis

Ababa to Nairobi. Then on into the bush by Land Rover. Ruark describes what it was like to wake on his first morning in the jungle, so very far from his New York apartment (he has just heard a lion nearby):

> It had been such a swift transition from New York to a lion in your lap. Philip Wiley, I believe it was, once wrote that when you travel by plane you leave a little of your soul behind. I figured in my semi-sleep that a part of my soul was somewhere between Rome and Asmara, which is in Eritrea and which might stay right there in Eritrea for all of me. Or maybe it was just now trying to check into the second-worst hotel in Addis Ababa . . .
>
> The lion coughed now, quite close. The birds and the insects and the baboons set up a new symphony. By dead reckoning I estimated that my soul was just getting off the Ethiopia plane in Nairobi.[1]

Those of you who have experienced the so-called jet lag of international travel can relate—when you travel by plane it does feel like you have left a little of your soul behind, and it often takes days for your soul to catch up. Ruark's account is charming because it feels antiquated. A swift transition? It took him almost two *weeks* to reach the bush; I flew nonstop from Atlanta to Johannesburg in fifteen hours. But I appreciate someone saying it is jarring to jump from one reality to another without much transition.

I, too, remember my first night in the bush. The jackals woke me up with their eerie cackles, so different from the American coyote, so "other." The sound unnerved me as I lay on my cot in the dark, bleary with jet lag, my soul still somewhere over the Atlantic. Breakfast was served at what felt like seven in the evening to my body—seven o'clock the night before. We rushed out into our own African adventure—two days bow-hunting kudu jammed before a business trip—but the whole thing felt terribly wrong. This was not how I wanted to experience Africa. The rhythm wasn't right at all.

LOSING ALL SENSE OF TIMING

Stasi and I attended the memorial service of a family friend this fall, a beautiful young man whose life was cut short in his twenties. Those are such awful, poignant occasions, filled with so many conflicting emotions. The hugs, the whispered conversations, the tears with many people who are themselves reeling in various ways. His service was beautiful and heartbreaking. Our family needed to be together afterward—you can't just go home after something like this—so we had planned on lunch. But I simply could not make that transition quickly. While most of the congregation filed quietly out of the church, I sat in my chair looking out the window, allowing my tears to continue, not requiring myself to bounce back. To rise up for the conversations I knew were waiting in the hallway outside. My soul needed God, and he was waiting right there for me in a more gracious transition.

I think it was Archibald Hart who pointed out that because we are so accustomed to moving pedal to the metal in our own world, the thing we overlook in the Gospels are all of the in-between times when Christ and his followers were walking from one town to another. When the record states, "The next day Jesus decided to leave for Galilee" (John 1:43), we project our own pace upon it, not realizing it took the boys *three days by foot* to get there. Three days just strolling along, talking, or sharing the silent beauty; the pauses for lunch or a drink from a well; the campfires in the evening. Even as I write this, it sounds luxurious. Christ does not move immediately from one dramatic story to another; there was down time, transition time between those demands. Time to process what had happened (these are the moments you see the disciples asking questions; "what did you mean by . . . ?"). Time to catch their breath before the next encounter.

That was the pace Jesus felt was reasonable for people engaged in important things *and* wanting a life with God. Time we would categorize almost as vacation time, for those are the only periods we allow ourselves a stroll, a lingering lunch, a campfire conversation. We highly progressive moderns try to keep up without any of those intervals and transitions.

The things that we require of ourselves—we go from a tender conversation with our eight-year-old anxious about going to school to an angry phone call with our insurance company as we drive to work, followed by a quick chat with our sister needing a decision about our aging parents' "memory care unit." Then it's straight into a series of business meetings (during which we multitask by trying to bang out some email), firing an employee, interviewing another, making dinner reservations for our spouse's birthday, fitting in a conversation with our boss because we can't say no, and showing up late and haggard for the dinner.

And we wonder why we have a hard time finding God, receiving more of him, feeling like we're overflowing with life.

The EMT, who leaves the scene of a terrible accident, races to get to his Bible study group, but wonders afterward why he couldn't find God there. The schoolteacher, who comes home exhausted from a day herding a riotous classroom, tries to be present to her own child, but can't seem to find the right gear to do so. The modern pastor, who needs to be a real estate expert in one meeting, a brilliant trauma counselor in the next, and a caring friend over lunch, only to shift gears into the role of savvy corporate CEO for the meeting that follows.

We are forcing our souls through multiple gear-changes each day, each *hour*, and after years of this we wonder why we aren't even sure what to say when a friend genuinely inquires, "How are you?" We don't really know; we aren't sure what we feel anymore. We live at one speed: go. All the subtleties of human experience have been forced into one state of being.

Mercy. No soul was meant to live like this.

What sort of madness have we come to accept as normal when a One Minute Pause feels like a luxury?!

RECOVERING TRANSITIONS

Your soul is the vessel God fills, yet there is no room for him to fill if your soul is wrung out, twisted, haggard, fried. Put another way, your hands cannot receive a gift while they are still tightly clenched. That is the condition we are trying to recover from and avoid further commerce with. Which brings us to how important transitions are as an expression of kindness.

When our boys were young, we established a family tradition of a summer vacation in the Tetons. Rivers, lakes, mountains, ice cream, wildlife—like summer camp, but everything suited to our own desires. Precious memories. Now our sons are raising families of their own, busy with their careers and church communities, and those trips are harder and harder to come by.

Last summer we were able to pull off a return, this time with an armada of strollers, car seats, and portable cribs. We had a wonderful time, and it passed far too quickly. Because of the demands on their lives, our children needed to fly straight home. But Stasi and I chose to drive, to set a gracious pace over our return. We further intentionally broke the drive up with a night in a small Wyoming town we love, at a charming little motel along the Wind River.

Sure, we could have gotten home in two hours, not two days, had we also flown. We could have made the road trip a direct push and made it home the same day. But we have learned that to yank our souls out of wilderness, beauty, family, joy, and happiness in order to hurl ourselves back into our world is simply violent. We are choosing to recognize the importance of *transitions*.

Do you allow a grace of transitions in your life, or do you simply blast from one thing to the next?

When the technological revolution of the twentieth century was taking place, led by the development of the microchip, the human race watched breathlessly as breakthrough upon breakthrough accelerated computer design and how quickly we could process information. (The first computer was the size of a small house; now you carry its capacity in your hand.) Which led to breakthroughs in communication, commerce, travel. (By "breakthroughs," what we primarily meant was *faster*; we were able to do everything so much faster.) Technology was going to make our lives easier, make room for doing the things we love.

Exactly the opposite has taken place.

Technology took over our lives to be sure, but instead of creating more room for living, we have had to force ourselves to run to the dizzying pace of technology. (Notice how irritated you are when your computer takes ten seconds to boot up instead of two. Or when you can't access your favorite app because at the moment you don't have a cell signal.) Without thinking, we simply expect our souls to process information and communications as quickly as computers and mobile devices. "Electronic mail" replaced actual handwritten letters; texting replaced email. But texts have proven too cumbersome (can you believe it?), so we resort to the emoji. A tiny cartoon face to let our loved ones know we are surprised, or embarrassed, angry, happy, sad. Supremely efficient, and utterly stripped of humanity. This is progress? Honestly—you can't stop long enough to write an actual reply?

(It appears even the emoji is too much effort now; my friends have all resorted to replying to a text with a "like" exclamation point, or the equally banal "ha ha" instant reply device. This isn't even communication; we are grunting at one another like cavemen.)

I worked in Washington, DC, in the late '80s. My daily commute was by train; I could read or look out the window. I couldn't do email, check the latest news feed, update my status, text anyone. I arrived home disentangled from the intense life of the Hill and much better able to be present to my family and friends and nonwork life. Technology—and the resulting assault on our attention—has robbed us of ordinary transition spaces and opportunities. As soon as there is a down moment, everyone is back on their phones. Myself included.

I was at the department of motor vehicles the other day, updating a car registration. Realizing it would be some time before I was served, I instinctively reached for my phone. Then I stopped and chose to simply sit. Look around. Breathe a little. People watch. It was alarming to me how much discipline it took. We truly don't know what to do with downtime any more.

DIVINE DISRUPTION

My sons have taken up triathlons (where athletes compete in a multi-discipline race typically composed of running, cycling, and swimming).

They explained the margin of victory is often made up in the transitions: when the athlete leaves the water and needs to get to their bike, often strip off a wetsuit, pull on bike shoes and helmet, and get pedaling as quickly as possible. The goal is to do all this while still moving, stripping as they leave the water, etc. This is precisely the attitude we've taken to the events of our lives. The problem is, in a triathlon transitions are meant to be whittled down to nothing. But that's not true for those gracious spaces between the events of human living.

I wonder—how many situations that we would call "disappointments," "hassles," and "setbacks" might actually be the loving hand of God trying to slow us down for the sake of our souls, and so that we might receive him?

Friends were recently on vacation in Mexico. Eight lovely days to celebrate their anniversary. The weather was glorious sunshine until their last full day, when it rained cats and dogs for twenty-four hours. No chance to get to the beach. Just stay inside and read. They felt disappointed, felt their last day was being robbed—until they realized how gracious this was of God to prepare them to let go of what felt like paradise and return to their demanding worlds, leaving golden beaches, flip-flops, and eighty-three degrees for snow and sleet back in the Northwest. God provided a transition day to allow their hearts a more gentle change.

I believe that God is often providing the opportunity for transition, but since we don't have eyes to see it we may have been missing it.

A friend of mine was on his way home from a business trip. Rushing through the airport, trying to get a standby seat on an earlier flight, he had a whopper of an argument with his wife on the phone. He did not get the standby seat and was delayed several hours. First he simply sulked; the anger which lingered from his argument with his spouse carried over into his travel woes. He later realized God was in the delay—that he needed those hours in the airport, first to cool off, then to realize the argument was mostly because he demands his wife live at the furious pace he does. Those hours provided room to process that realization, to get time enough with God to allow his soul to come to the grace of repentance, and to call his wife back. All that lovely redemption would have been missed if he had been allowed to continue what he considered simply the normal pace of an ordinary day.

Our souls need transition time. Especially in this world. We will find God in the transitions. Notice that in the Gospels, it was during those transition times the disciples got to have Jesus to themselves; the intimacy was in those moments. God is in the mission too; of course he is. He meets us in crisis and action. But there is a sweetness to the downtime, even if it is brief. We can find more of God there.

GIVING IT A TRY

We practice kindness. We intentionally create space for transitions.

The One Minute Pause is a wonderful tool. I'm learning to use it in the midst of busy days, when I would normally just hit "launch" as I walk out the door in the morning, and blast all day like the space shuttle from meeting to phone call to writing something to conversation to lunch and back at it again. It is new for me—and so gracious to my soul—to pause after I hang up the phone and before I turn right back to email or make another call; pause after one meeting before I go into another; pause when I arrive at work after my morning commute; and pause when I pull into the driveway at the end of my day.

If you have five minutes waiting time, don't look at your phone. Just . . . be. Look around; people watch.

When planning events like holidays or vacations, or coming demands such as a memorial service we must attend, create a little space for the transition needed before and after. Especially after.

Let's be honest—we will need to loosen our grasp on efficiency. Efficiency is often what drives us to remove all margin from our lives. To fill every moment. It is especially hard on our relationships.

Efficiency is the "how" of life: how we meet and handle the demands of daily living, how we survive, grow, and create, how we deal with stress, how effective we are in our functional roles and activities.

In contrast, love is the "why" of life: why we are functioning at all, what we want to be efficient *for*. . . .

Love should come first; it should be the beginning of and the reason for everything. Efficiency should be "how" love expresses its "why." But it gets mixed up so easily. When I was a young parent, I wanted to take good care *of* my children (efficiency) because

I cared so much *for* them (love). But I soon became preoccupied with efficiency. What were my kids eating? Where they getting enough sleep? Would we be on time for the car pool? My concerns about efficiency began to eclipse the love they were meant to serve. Getting to the carpool on time became more important than attending to a small fear or a hurt feeling. Too often the report card—the preeminent symbol of childhood efficiency—was more significant than the hopes and fears of the little one who brought it home. It happens to all of us.[2]

So—we embrace a little inefficiency in our lives. So what if you are late to the carpool? It's not a massive issue. So what if people have to wait an extra day for you to reply to their email? It's good for you, and it's probably good for them.

And when the hard stuff hits—the unexpected news, the delay, the setback—we practice kindness. Just today I was looking forward to my writing time. I had several hours blocked out in the afternoon to work on this book. But when I came home there were some troubling messages from credit card companies; after a few calls we learned our identity had been compromised. We had to make a number of calls to try to stop the hemorrhaging. We got things worked out, but it was stressful and upsetting. That done, I needed to resume my work as an author. Life carries on. But my soul was not ready. So I allowed some space for transition. I played some worship music while I simply sat in my office. And when I did turn to work, I began with simple tasks like checking research, picking up some lost notes. Kindness. Transition.

seven

GET OUTSIDE

One of the best things that happened to me this summer was the air conditioning going out in my truck. That truck's got a hundred sixty thousand miles on it, so I wasn't too upset. The shutdown forced me to drive with the windows down, which opened the world to me in a way I didn't even know I needed. They called it "Texas air conditioning" back in the day; cars used to come equipped with little triangular windows on both the driver and passenger sides, which flipped inward; people used them to force air in. You don't see those anymore because we prefer driving sealed in our little shell. As Robert Pirsig wrote in his '70s classic, *Zen and the Art of Motorcycle Maintenance,*

> In a car you're always in a compartment, and because you're used to it you don't realize that through that car window everything you see is just more TV. You're a passive observer and it is all moving by you boringly in a frame.[1]

Driving with the windows down required me to drive a little slower, a good thing in itself, which allowed me to take in all the wonderful aromas of summer—hayfields, pine forest, wet pavement after a shower, rivers (yes, rivers have a very distinct fragrance; some coastal rivers smell like a bad fish market, but the rivers flowing down from high mountains have a lovely aroma I would call "forest nectar" or "green freshness"). I got to enjoying it so much I didn't get the air fixed for months.

PLASTIC WRAP

The opening of the twenty-first century has seen some pretty alarming headlines: 9/11; Katrina; Afghanistan; ethnic cleansing in Sudan; ISIS, Syria; various bombings and earthquakes; the global refugee crisis.

Then I ran across a news release so shocking I had to read it twice. It didn't make the front page, but it should have: the average person now spends 93 percent of their life indoors (this includes your transportation time in car, bus, or metro).[2] Ninety-three percent— such a staggering piece of information. We should pause for a moment and let the tragedy sink in.

That means if you live to be 100, you will have spent 93 of those years in a little compartment and only 7 outside in the dazzling, living world. If we live to the more usual 75, we will spend 69 and three-fourths of our years indoors, and only 5 and one-fourth outside. This includes our childhood; how does a child be a child when they only venture outside a few months of their entire childhood?

This is a catastrophe, the final nail in the coffin for the human soul. You live nearly all your life in a fake world: artificial lighting instead of the warmth of sunlight or the cool of moonlight or the darkness of night itself. Artificial climate rather than the wild beauty of real weather; your world is always 68 degrees. All the surfaces you touch are things like plastic, nylon, and faux leather instead of meadow, wood, and stream. Fake fireplaces; wax fruit. The atmosphere you inhabit is now asphyxiating with artificial smells—mostly chemicals and "air fresheners"—instead of cut grass, wood smoke, and salt air (is anyone weeping yet?). In place of the cry of the hawk, the thunder of a waterfall, and the comfort of crickets, your world spews out artificial sounds—all the clicks and beeps and whir of technology, the hum of the HVAC. Dear God, even the plants in your little bubble are fake. They give no oxygen; instead the plastic off-gases toxins, and if that isn't a signal fire I don't know what is.

This is a life for people in a science fiction novel. This would be understandable, acceptable, if we'd colonized Mars and by necessity you lived in a bubble. But this is not the life God ordained for the sons of Adam and the daughters of Eve, whose habitat is this sumptuous earth. It's like putting wild horses in a Styrofoam box for the rest of their lives.

You live a bodily existence. The physical life, with all the glories of senses, appetites, and passions—this is the life God meant for us. It's through our senses we learn most every important lesson. Even in spiritual acts of worship and prayer we are standing or kneeling, engaging bodily. God put your soul in this amazing body and then put you in a world perfectly designed for that experience.

Which is why the rescue of the soul takes place through our engagement with the real world. Thus the quote—variously attributed to Churchill, Will Rogers, and Reagan—that "The best thing for the inside of a man is the outside of a horse." Because when we encounter an actual horse—not online, not through Instagram, not the little horse emoji on your phone, but a living, breathing, thousand-pound animal, we are thrust into a dynamic encounter with the real. It calls things out of us, not only fears, anger, and impatience to be overcome, but intuition and presence and a sort of firm kindness that no video game can ever replicate. There's no switch you can flip; you must engage. Reality shapes us.

I love world-class soccer ("football" in every country but the US); I can watch hours of it in a stretch. But I feel bleary-headed afterwards, foggy and disoriented, like a bird that hit a window. Just compare how you feel after binge-watching hours of screen anything—TV, video games, YouTube—with how you feel when you come off a mountain bike ride or a swim in the ocean. Living in an artificial world is like spending your life wrapped in plastic wrap. You wonder why you feel tired, numb, a little depressed, when the simple answer is you have a vitamin D deficiency; there's no sunlight in your life, literally and figuratively.

Our body, soul, and spirit atrophy because we were made to inhabit a real world, drawing life, joy, and strength from it. To be shaped by it, to relish in it. Living your days in an artificial world is like living your whole life with gloves on, a filtered experience, never really feeling anything. Then you wonder why your soul feels numb.

GOD IS OUT THERE

We are looking for more of God. You're far more likely to find him in a walk through an orchard or a sit by a pond than you are in a subway terminal. Of course God is with us and for us wherever we are, but in terms of refreshment, renewal, *restoration*, in terms of finding God in ways we can drink deeply of his wonderful being, you'd do better to look for him in the cry of the gull than the scream of the siren. God inhabits the world he made; his vibrancy permeates all creation:

> The whole earth is filled with his glory! (Isaiah 6:3 NLT)

> Christ . . . ascended higher than all the heavens, so that he might fill the entire universe with himself. (Ephesians 4:9–10 NLT)

In the most beloved of Psalms, perhaps the most beloved of all scripture, David wrote a poem to celebrate the restoration of his soul. Notice that God took him into nature to accomplish that:

> The LORD is my shepherd, I lack nothing.
> He makes me lie down in green pastures,

> he leads me beside quiet waters,
>
> he refreshes my soul. (Psalm 23:1–3)

Be careful you don't dismiss this as something belonging to an agrarian age. God could have taken David into the palace to renew him; he could have taken him into the home of a friend or family member; he could have chosen the bustling markets of Jerusalem. In other words, there were plenty of indoor options for God to employ. But his choice for David's resuscitation was nature, his greenhouse, filled with his own life, pulsing with his glory, unique in its ability to restore and renew his children.

"The world is charged with the grandeur of God," wrote the Jesuit poet Gerard Manley Hopkins.[3] It follows that we should have no problem finding more of God out there, receiving that grand glory into our own being, like the deer panting for water. But by 1877 something had happened to our relationship with the garden world we've been given as our home. . . .

> Generations have trod, have trod, have trod;
>
> And all is seared with trade; bleared, smeared with toil;
>
> And wears man's smudge and shares man's smell: the soil
>
> Is bare now, nor can foot feel, being shod.[4]

The world had become "modernized," mechanized, the grandeur smeared and smudged in our race to make our lives more efficient. Mankind had begun to prefer the "gloved" life, shod, a further step removed from the healing power God offers through the outside world. Even so—and here's proof of the resiliency of creation saturated in God's glory—Hopkins knew the gift could be recovered.

> And for all this, nature is never spent;
> There lives the dearest freshness deep down things;
> And though the last lights off the black West went
> Oh, morning, at the brown brink eastward, springs—
> Because the Holy Ghost over the bent
> World broods with warm breast and with ah! bright wings.[5]

The rescue is always close at hand. The Spirit of God still hovers over creation; nature is ever renewed with "the dearest freshness." There's nothing better for a fried soul than to get in the woods or walk in the park. Lie on your back in the grass and watch the clouds go by. Sit on the beach and watch the breakers.

I've been enjoying the memoir *H is for Hawk* by Helen Macdonald, a Cambridge researcher who recovers a childhood love of hawks at a critical moment when it seems her world is collapsing around her. Ensconced in the urbane society of Oxbridge, she begins her story with a siren call to her barbequed soul:

> At five in the morning I've been staring at a square of streetlight
> on the ceiling, listening to a couple of late party-leavers chatting
> on the pavement outside. I felt odd: overtired, overwrought,
> unpleasantly like my brain had been removed and my skull stuffed

with something like microwaved aluminum foil, dented, charred and shorting with sparks. *Nnngh. Must get out*, I thought, throwing back the covers. *Out!* I pulled on jeans, boots and a jumper, scalded my mouth with burned coffee, and it was only when my frozen, ancient Volkswagen and I were halfway down the A14 that I worked out where I was going, and why. Out there, beyond the foggy windscreen and white lines was the forest. . . . That's where I was headed. To see goshawks.[6]

Drawn, *compelled* to the woods just an hour from the city, she transitions into nature, and good things begin to happen for her soul:

For so long I'd been living in libraries and college rooms, frowning at screens, marking essays, chasing down academic references. This was a different kind of hunt. Here I was a different animal. Have you ever watched a deer walking out from cover? They step, stop, and stay, motionless, nose to the air, looking and smelling. A nervous twitch might run down their flanks. And then, reassured that all is safe, they ankle their way out of the brush to graze. That morning, I felt like the deer. . . . Something inside me ordered me how and where to step without me knowing much about it. On my goshawk hunt I feel tense when I'm walking or standing in sunlight, find myself unconsciously edging towards broken light, or slipping into the narrow, cold shadows along the wide breaks between pine stands.[7]

She's tuning in. Her soul is breaking from the cocoon that life in an artificial world muffles us in:

> I was looking down at a little sprig of Mahonia growing out of the turf, it's oxblood leaves like buffed pigskin. I glanced up. And then I saw my goshawks. There they were. A pair, soaring above the canopy in the rapidly warming air. There was a flat, hot hand of sun on the back of my neck, but I smelt ice in my nose, seeing those goshawks soaring. I smelt ice and bracken stems and pine resin. . . . I sat down, tired and content.[8]

Being present to the woods requires something of us, something you can't rush the soul through. It demands transition and *presence*. Notice Macdonald is aligning herself with the woods and wildlife around her, and that aligning process is unwrinkling her soul, smoothing it out, soothing it. This is why my hurried African "safari" felt so wrong; I tried to force it into a few hours, like a trip to the mall.

ALLOWING NATURE TO HEAL

I had a similar experience to Macdonald's recently, my own tin-foil-brain, fried-soul kind of day. Only my rescue didn't take place until I had thrashed through most of the calamity. It was the kind of day when everything seems to go sideways from the moment you get out of bed; I'll bet you've had one of these:

There's no milk, so there's no cereal, and you're late anyways, so there's no breakfast. You're halfway to work when you realize you forgot your phone—and who can live without their phone these days—so you're late to work because you went back and got your phone and now you're behind on everything. People are tweaked at you. You can't answer that urgent email someone keeps asking about, because you're waiting for an answer yourself, but the person who has the answer took the morning off for a "doctor's appointment" (*Sure you did*, you think, *you're out for a ride, you slouch*). On it goes.

You look forward to lunch as your first chance to come up for air, but the line at your favorite taco joint is out the door, and though you should have stayed, you're already well on your way to totally fried, so you leave in frustration, which only makes you skip lunch, which justifies your use of chocolate and caffeine to see you through the afternoon. But that completely takes your legs out from under you, and all you end up accomplishing is making a list of the things you need to do, which overwhelms you. By the time you get home, you are seriously fried.

I was strung out, deep in a vat of anger, frustration, self-indulging cynicism, and fatigue. A dangerous place to be. The next move would be rescue or the knockout punch. After a cold dinner I went out on the porch and just sat there. I knew I needed rescue, and I knew the nearest hope of that was the porch.

It was a beautiful Indian summer evening, the kind where the heat of the day has warmed the breezes, but you can also feel the cool from the mountains beginning to trickle down like refreshing streams. The crickets were going at it full bore, as they do when their season is about over, and the sunset was putting on a Western Art show. I could feel the rescue begin to enter my body and soul. Nature began its gentle work.

I let out a few deep sighs—"Spirit sighs," as a friend calls them, meaning your spirit is breathing in the Spirit of God and you find yourself letting go of all the mess, letting go of everything. They weren't cynical or defeated sighs; they were "letting it all go" sighs. My body relaxed, which made me realize how tense I'd been all day. My heart started coming to the surface, as it often does when I can get away into nature and let beauty have its effect on me. Mind you—I didn't get to the beach. I'm not canoeing some mountain lake. I'm simply sitting on my back porch. It doesn't take much; rescue is always at hand. Warm summer evening, cool breeze, beautiful sky now turning that deep navy blue just before dark, crickets making their eternal melodies.

That's when the carnival started.

A beer would make this a lot better, went the voice. *Or maybe tequila. You oughta go find some cookies.* Some agitated place in me started clamoring for relief. Even though the evening was washing over my soul, or maybe *because* it was allowing my soul to untangle, the carnival of desire started jockeying for my attention. *I think there's still some ice cream in the freezer.*

It felt like two kingdoms were vying for my soul. The carnival was offering relief. Nature was offering restoration. They are leagues apart, my friends. Leagues apart.

Relief is momentary; it's checking out, numbing, sedating yourself. Television is relief. Eating a bag of cookies is relief. Tequila is relief. And let's be honest—relief is what we reach for because it's immediate and usually within our grasp. Most of us turn there, when what we really need is *restoration*.

Nature heals; nature restores. Think of sitting on the beach watching the waves roll in at sunset and compare it to turning on the tube and vegging in front of *Narcos* or *Fear the Walking Dead*. The experiences could not be further apart. Remember how you feel sitting by a small brook, listening to its little musical songs, and contrast that to an hour of HALO. Video games offer relief; nature offers restoration.

This is what David was trying to put words to when he reported finding God in green meadows and beside quiet waters, emerging with a refreshed soul. Or as another translation has it, "He renews my strength" (Psalm 23:3 NLT). The world we live in fries the soul on a daily basis, fries it with a vengeance (it feels vengeful). We need the immersion David spoke of.

So I stayed on the porch, choosing to ignore the chorus of vendors trying to get me to leave in search of some relief (*Your favorite show is on; maybe what you want is wine . . .*). I knew if I left all I would find was sugar or alcohol, and my soul would be no better for it. So I chose to let the evening continue to have its healing ministry. Remember— God doesn't like to shout. His invitations are much more gentle.

Sunset was over; night was falling, and still I sat there. The evening itself was cool now, and an owl was hooting somewhere off in the distance. I could feel my soul settling down even more; the feeling was like unwrinkling or disentangling on a soul level, as your body does in a hot tub. *Thank you for this gift of beauty,* I said. *I receive it into my soul.*

Darkness, crickets, coolness, quiet. I felt like I'd been through detox. When I fell into bed that night, it was as if the hellish day had never even happened. Restoration. So much better than mere relief.

GIVING IT A TRY

Quite simply, get outside. As Van Gogh urged, "The great thing is to gather new vigor in reality."[9]

It doesn't have to be amazing; I'm not suggesting you have to get to the mountains or the ocean every morning (unless you live close by). I live three quarters of my year in pretty typical suburbs. But I've found a walk near my house, in a public space that has trees, trails, and a little stream. It's not much of a stream—more of a brook, a freshlet really. But it flows year-round, and I love visiting to watch what the stream is doing through the seasons. My ritual is to kneel and place my hand on the cold, glassy surface of the water, feeling it flow under my palm and around my hand. It's a startling summons back to the real, and always refreshing. Even in winter, when only little bubbles show a trace of the trickle under the ice, still I place my palm on the ice and let it sting and startle and remind me that the world is a very real thing.

Touch nature. I'm serious—every day, your soul needs to engage creation. There's all sorts of research showing how healing this is.[10] During the process of writing this book, I spent a good part of each day gazing into a computer screen, marking my own essays, chasing down references. My brain began to feel like sparking aluminum foil too. I kept having to get up, leave my office, and wander outside, simply to touch real things—stone, pinecones, the juniper bush. This wasn't a cognitive decision; it was a *compelling*, something I felt I had to do in order to come out from a weird ether-space, come back to myself. Yesterday, rain left our yard in a lightly moist condition. Laying my hand on a wet boulder, feeling the damp coolness, examining the granite crystals, I felt as though I'd returned to planet earth, like a character from outer space.

Get outside, every day. If you work out in a gym, take it outside with a run, bike, swim, hike. Turn off the AC and roll down the windows in your car. Walk around outside your office building every day. Feeling the sun on your face, a breath of wind, the fresh kiss of snowflakes is resuscitating. Technology—where most people live their lives—is draining. Nature is healing. So reduce one and increase the other.

Encounter weather whenever you can. Don't hide from it; experience it. I was on a two-week business trip recently; it began with an overnight flight, ten hours in a tube. From there it was airports, hotels, cars—an entirely artificial existence. Everything was fake—weather, lighting, sounds. I found myself increasingly wanting to drink, eat chocolate, watch TV. The artificial was wearing me down, poisoning me, and my soul was looking for quick relief. On the last night, a massive thunderstorm let loose in the city. My car was parked two blocks away. Instead of trying to avoid the rain by calling a cab, or cringing and moping at the fact that I would get utterly soaked, I *relished* it. I rejoiced the entire two torrential blocks; I whooped and shouted and let the rain utterly douse me. After days upon days in the artificial, it was a cleansing baptism. As C. S. Lewis wrote,

> To shrink back from all that can be called Nature into negative spirituality is as if we ran away from horses instead of learning to ride. . . . Who will trust me with a spiritual body if I cannot control even an earthly body? These small and perishable bodies we now have were given to us as ponies are given to schoolboys. We must learn to manage: not that we may someday be free of horses altogether but that someday we may ride bareback, confident and rejoicing, those greater mounts, those winged, shining and world-shaking horses which perhaps even now expect us with impatience, pawing and snorting in the King's stables.[11]

Nature heals, teaches, strengthens, soothes; it brings us the presence of God, for "The whole earth is filled with his glory" (Isaiah 6:3 NLT). Go let it restore your soul—daily, whenever possible.

eight

REMEMBERING WHO YOU LOVE

I received a text the other day from a friend of mine. It began as a surprising intrusion of joy, which grew into a rescue of my soul.

First came simply a photo, taken from the window of a bush plane somewhere in the Alaskan wilderness. At first glance, I couldn't quite make out what I was looking at. All I could see was a massive mountain slope, angling down toward a river. The impression was something far north and exotic. There are no trees in the photo, only tundra in autumn colors. The picture was taken from probably seventeen thousand feet, and something is dappling the surface of the tundra on both sides of the river. As my eyes adjusted, I realized I was looking at a massive assembly of living creatures, something out of Eden. While my mind tried to take in and sort out what I was beholding, the second text followed: "ninety thousand caribou stacked up for a river crossing." It filled my heart with joy—not only because I love wildness and massive animal migrations, but because it reminded me of the God I love.

And oh, how good it is to be reminded of the God we love—what he's really like, how generous his heart is.

I had a similar experience a few evenings later when Stasi and I were watching a BBC nature series on the oceans of our planet. Richly filmed in high definition, intimate and epic, the vast, colorful beauty of the seas, coasts, and coral lagoons saturating this planet was enough to evoke worship during every episode. The seven seas are gorgeous; talk about abundance! This particular episode was shot in the open ocean (utterly breathtaking) and a massive pod of dolphins began to fill the screen. Fifty . . . one hundred . . . one thousand dolphins all racing along in the open sea, twisting, leaping, diving in a sort of organized, whimsical chaos, racing along in pure dolphin happiness. The narrator explained we were watching a "super pod" of Atlantic dolphins *five thousand strong*. I was speechless; such things exist?! That encounter, that revelation was so holy that it removed in the moment every doubt I had in the goodness of God. *Right. This is the God I love*, I thought to myself. And my heart came back to him in tender hopefulness and affection.

We are talking about finding more of God. I assure you nothing, absolutely nothing, will bring you more of him than loving him. Turning our hearts toward God in love opens our being to receive him like no other practice. And it is a practice, something we consciously and actively engage in through the moments of our day-to-day. This is the epicenter of the book, really. The core truth from which all others flow. But I saved this chapter till now for several reasons . . .

Most of my readers will be people of faith backgrounds, and as such, you have heard so many messages about love, loving God, God is love, that your soul has formed a kind of callous to the beauty of what such words reveal. We are too familiar with the conversation—almost, dare we admit, a little bored with it. So I waited until now to try unlocking this treasure because your soul needed some time to recover and heal through the practices we've looked at. We also needed the transition the preceding chapters have provided to help us disentangle from the world (including the religious world, which runs at basically the same pace as the rest of the mad world).

But I mostly forestalled this moment, this most essential of all truths, because our souls have built up some resistance to it through the disappointments of our lives, and we need to proceed with gentleness if we might open this, the greatest gift of all.

LOVING WHO? WHY?

I mentioned that our beloved Golden Retriever was dying; we lost him in November. A few weeks earlier, one of our horses sustained a near-fatal injury. I feared we would lose him too. Those were only a few of the sorrows that came into our lives this year; others were even worse. It caused my heart to question God's love for me—sorrow always does. As does suffering and chronic disappointment. The heart reacts by pulling away, not perhaps so far as to abandon faith, but still . . . something gets in. Some wounded doubt about his goodness and, more pointedly, his goodness toward *us* in particular.

Life has a way of eroding our confidence in the goodness of God. What a ridiculous understatement; let me try again. Life is a savage assault, striking at random, poisoning our heart's assurance that God is good, or at least good toward us. This makes it so hard to find more of God, to receive him in fresh and wonderful ways into our being. So it's here we must seek healing, and now is a good time to do so.

Allow me to explain an essential dynamic to the soul's relationship with God. Then perhaps we can gently open our own souls to the exquisite experience.

More of God comes to us as we love God. The more that we love God, the more we are able to experience him. Part of this has to do with the nature of God, and part of it has to do with our own human nature.

You understand from your own relationships, your story of love, that you don't give your heart away to just anyone. You don't give access to the deeper places in your soul to just any idle acquaintance— certainly not to someone who is at the same time keeping themselves distant from you. We know from our own experiences that when someone loves us, we are much more ready to make ourselves available to them. What we keep forgetting is that God feels the same way.

For the eyes of the LORD range throughout the earth to strengthen those whose hearts are fully committed to him. (2 Chronicles 16:9)

The LORD says, "I will rescue those who love me." (Psalm 91:14 NLT)

The Father himself loves you because you have loved me. (John 16:27)

I'm really surprised that the human race expects God to pour himself and his blessings into their lives when he is not even the slightest priority, let alone a close and dear friend. Would you give the best of your life to people who couldn't care less whether or not you exist? God's outpouring of himself is *conditional*. I know, I know—we've been told all about the unconditional love of God. Absolutely—his *grace* is unconditional; his forgiveness is available to all. However, *intimacy* with him, the treasures of his presence, the outpouring of his vibrant being into our thirsty souls—that's for those who love him. Even in the best friendship, the act of giving and receiving love ebbs and flows with the willingness of the two involved to make it a priority, to invest themselves. God's heart is very much like yours in this way, for your heart is made in his image.

One of the things I love about horses is that they don't let you get away with much. If I show up to the stables hurried and distracted, and therefore try to rush my horses through a time of interaction, they don't cooperate. If I'm angry, they pick up on that; if I don't really want to be there, they sense that too. Horses exist outside the mad world, so if you would enjoy the riches of a life with them, you can't insist they enter your madness. And good for them. Of course they shouldn't; they deserve more. To enjoy the fellowship of a horse, you have to step into their world, and they are happy to meet you there. Which is yet another of nature's expressions of the heart of God. Whether or not you currently, in-this-moment love him matters to him. Very much.

Now on our side of the exchange, loving God opens our soul up to the presence of God and the gifts he has for us. Remember—your soul is the vessel he fills. We're trying to use these practices to help position our souls into the place whereby we might receive so much more of God. There's no practice that facilitates the opening of our capacity to perceive him, and receive him, like the turning of our hearts and souls toward God in love. *Active* loving—love as a verb, not a noun. This is what we're made for, and the soul knows it, even if it's long been unused. We know it even though we've pulled back in sorrow or disappointment.

I love how our wildflowers track the course of the sun through the sky, slowly turning to face the warm, passing brightness from east to west in such a sweet act of humble adoration. Many flowers fold their petals inward come evening, through the chilly nights at seven thousand feet, then open again with the rising of the sun and turn its direction. "Hearts unfold like flowers before thee," goes the great "Hymn of Joy," "opening to the sun above."

> Melt the clouds of sin and sadness;
> drive the dark of doubt away.
> Giver of immortal gladness,
> fill us with the light of day![1]

That's it—we need the clouds of sin and sadness melted away; we need the dark of our doubts driven off like night flees before dawn. So that the giver of immortal gladness might *fill us*. Two simple practices will help you get there.

BRINGING OUR HEARTS BACK AROUND

Start with something you love. The laughter of your child. Sunlight on the ocean. Your beloved dog. A favorite song, music itself. Perhaps a photo, like my caribou. A favorite spot—your garden, the cliffs at the sea, the family cabin. Someone dear to you. We begin with the things we love; this is the way back, the path home. For we don't always draw the connection—God made these specifically for you, and he gave you the heart to love them. You'll be out for a bike ride in the very early morning, cool breeze in your face, all the sweet, fresh aromas it brings, the exhilaration of speed, and your heart spontaneously sings, *I love this!* The next step is to say, *So does God. He made this moment; he made these things. He is the creator of everything I love.* Your heart will naturally respond by opening toward him.

It's like throwing your faith a lifeline: Every wonderful thing in your life is a gift from God, an expression of his heart toward you. All your precious memories, each and every one—your eighth birthday, when you got that little red bike that awakened your love of riding, which carried right on into your adult life. That perfect powder day, when you and your fiancé skied run after run, then warmed up by the fire in the lodge. The vacation you still think about, how fun it was, how carefree you felt. Your wedding reception: the dancing, the inextinguishable joy of it all. Every moment you have ever been happy, thrilled, comforted, hopeful . . . that was God loving you. Such gifts come from no other source. "You open your hand and satisfy the desires of every living thing. . . . Every good and perfect gift is from above, coming down from the Father" (Psalm 145:16; James 1:17).

No other act will bring you a greater measure of God than loving him, actively engaging your heart and soul in loving him. Because as we do, the flower of our being opens up to the sunshine of his presence and all the goodness he longs to breathe into us. The best way to get there is to think upon the things we love and remind ourselves, "This is from God; this is his true heart."

Because life is a savage assault on our heart's confidence that God is good—and thus our union with him—the practice of reminding ourselves he is the creator of everything we love will be a rescue of our faith.

Now, I'm not trying to put a Band-Aid over deep sorrow, suffering, trauma, or loss. Not for a moment. I'm not pretending that what those things have done to your relationship with God can be healed in a moment. But you'll be astonished and delighted by how much *can* be recovered in this practice. And there is another practice that you will find equally helpful:

Love God in your suffering.

Stay with me now. Your heart is the greatest treasure you have. Without a heart it's impossible to love, or receive love. Without a heart you can't possibly dream, hope, laugh, find courage. Without a heart you will never be happy. Your enemy knows this, knows he can use your suffering to both shut your heart down and turn you against God, if only subtly, in doubtful hurt. Listen to me carefully: *You must not let him.* You must guard your heart with everything you've got, especially in times of disappointment and pain. Your secret weapon against the enemy's hatred is to love God right then and there, in the midst of the sorrow, whatever it may be.

I recognize that the act of loving God often surfaces other things in our hearts, things that are currently in the way of our loving him. We might feel half-hearted in the act, and then we realize we feel hurt or distant from God, or that he feels distant from us. This is good; this allows us to bring to the surface and put words to things that are blocking the relationship. Naming those things is important. I will at this point either begin to write about it in my journal or simply say to Jesus, "I feel hurt about . . ." Then I will pray, "Come into this hurt, this feeling of abandonment, this numbness," or whatever seems to be thwarting our intimacy. "I love you here, God. I choose right here, in this, to love you."

Try it; you'll see.

I realize that sometimes these roadblocks are quite significant and may require more serious attention. You might need to process it with a counselor, or ask your spiritual leaders for prayer. But you want to work out the problems *while staying in the relationship*, not backing away from it—just like a married couple or good friends have to do. You bring it up, sort it out, by staying in conversation with the other person. Even if you feel you can't sort it out right now, you stay present to the dialogue instead of leaving the country. Your intimacy with God, this heart-to-heart love we were made for, this is *the* thing Satan most hates, and it has to be fought for. Not just by God, by the way; don't wait for him to make it better. Far too many people react to God in adolescent anger, like Elsa in *Frozen*. We must live maturely, knowing that whatever else is happening, we must preserve the relationship if we would find our way.

When I'm feeling more disappointment than I am overflowing with reasons to love God, I turn to the things I know he has done on my behalf. "Thank you for creation," I'll say, because I love the world he's made, and I can at least start there—the meadows, waterfalls, caribou, dolphins.

"Thank you for creation." I continue, "Thank you for redemption"—for I know he loves me because of Jesus Christ: "God showed his great love for us by sending Christ to die for us while we were still sinners" (Romans 5:8 NLT). "Thank you for my redemption." And I will add, "Thank you for the coming kingdom," because it reminds me that my dreams *will* come true, any day now; goodness *is* coming to me. So when I'm trying to bring my heart along into the genuine act of loving God, I will pray, "Thank you for creation; thank you for redemption; thank you for the coming Kingdom." My soul comes along as I do this, and I remember that I do in fact love God, whatever my current heartache may be.

This rescue helps your heart not pull away from the One Person who can heal you; it fortresses your heart against the lies of the enemy that rush in during heartbreak (*God doesn't love you; he's not good; you are alone; life is unfair*—all that). Actively choosing to love God in our pain allows us to receive the very grace the pain cries out for.

Let me give you an example. Some dear friends lost a child. That story is not mine to tell here. What I can say is that in their grief, they began to love God. "We still love you, God. We declare that you are good." All heaven was breathless; all hell was screeching in horror. Because they took away the enemy's weapon and turned it against him. It wasn't easy; there were still floods of tears. But they were not bitter tears, not angry or cynical, because they kept their hearts open to the One who could carry them through. Too many people pull away, walk through their pain alone, making it all the worse and lengthy. I can report that my friends' healing from the loss was much quicker because they chose this path, for it kept their souls open to God's presence, and he was, therefore, able to offer himself in healing love. They made an offering of their suffering.

Make an offering of your suffering. Love God in it.

GIVING IT A TRY

This isn't complicated. We simply start saying, "I love you" as we turn our attention toward him for a moment or two. As I do so I find it helpful to recall some reason I love God: his goodness, the beauty of the world (ninety thousand caribou stacked up for a river crossing), a kindness I recently received. "God is the creator of everything

I love." Just repeat that to yourself, "God is the creator of everything I love."

Reminding yourself that God is the one who brought into existence the very things *you* love is a wonderful reminder to your soul of the intimacy between God's heart and yours. You love the same things! Did you know that? Close friends love the same things; lovers love the same things. Go on and think of something else that delights your heart—laughter, beauty, your favorite things in nature, a childhood fairytale. Beginning with the things we love is the way back toward God.

As you go through your normal day, practice saying "I love you" to God. Not once, but repeating it as you turn your heart toward him. Saying "I love you"—either out loud or quietly in the sanctuary of our inner life—causes our heart to follow; our being begins to enter into the *act* of loving. We turn our thoughts toward him— our Father, or Jesus, or the Holy Spirit. We turn toward him in the pauses of our day.

In loving him, we are able to receive him. As we receive him, we realize again how wonderful he truly is. Our heart enlarges for him, our union is strengthened, and we can receive more of him.

RETURNING TO THE
ONE MINUTE PAUSE

We've traveled enough distance now to be able to make better use of the One Minute Pause. You've got a grasp on benevolent detachment, taking back your attention, allowing the grace of transition, the goodness of loving God actively. This will make your experience of the pause all the better. Here's what it looks like for the practiced . . .

First, as we enter our pause, we release; we know now that we can't find God when we're distracted, burdened, hostage to so much noise. So what we do is simply give it all over; we let it all go. We practice benevolent detachment:

I give everyone and everything to you, God.
I give everyone, and everything to you.

Repeat it over and over. You'll know in the moment what to release—a person, a conversation, a project, the world. Release, and pause. If you find you need help releasing something, ask for his help!

Help me release, God. I give it all to you.

Next, we ask God for union with him:

Father, Jesus, Holy Spirit—restore my union with you.
Renew our union. I pray for union; I pray for oneness.

I'll repeat that a bit, too, lingering with it.
Then we practice actively loving God:

I love you, God. I believe you. I worship you.
I love you, I believe you, I worship you.

And we ask for more of God:

Fill me with so much more of you. I need so much more of you.

Are you working the Pause into your day? Download the One Minute Pause app from the app store. It's a beautiful and gentle guide through the practice, and you can set daily reminders for yourself in the app!

nine

SURRENDERING THE SELF LIFE

Here you are, humming right along—chapter 9! You're taking your soul back from the frenzied, whirling-dervish world. Gaining some detachment by turning your burdens over to the One you love. You're allowing the grace of transition, letting beauty and nature soothe your damaged soul! I hope you're finding the sweet relief these graces bring. Coming home to God is such a relief; there's simply no other place human beings can flourish as we were meant to. Especially in this hour. Well done!

Now, there's something lurking up ahead: a subtle trap waiting to trip you up, diminish your entire experience. Exposing it, and getting rid of it, is going to be a *profound* relief.

We begin to uncover this hidden downfall through something revealed in the parable of the prodigal son—though probably not in the character you're thinking of. Let's catch up on the unfolding drama as the younger son has just returned from his destructive lifestyle, and the father is giving orders . . .

The father said to his servants, "Quick! Bring the best robe and put it on him. Put a ring on his finger and sandals on his feet. Bring the fattened calf and kill it. Let's have a feast and celebrate. For this son of mine was dead and is alive again; he was lost and is found." So they began to celebrate.

Meanwhile, the older son was in the field. When he came near the house, he heard music and dancing. So he called one of the servants and asked him what was going on. "Your brother has come," he replied, "and your father has killed the fattened calf because he has him back safe and sound."

The older brother became angry and refused to go in. So his father went out and pleaded with him. But he answered his father, "Look! All these years I've been slaving for you and never disobeyed your orders. Yet you never gave me even a young goat so I could celebrate with my friends. But when this son of yours who has squandered your property with prostitutes comes home, you kill the fattened calf for him!"

"My son," the father said, "you are always with me, and everything I have is yours. But we had to celebrate and be glad, because this brother of yours was dead and is alive again; he was lost and is found." (Luke 15:22–32)

Something very unattractive is operating in the older brother; he can't go to his brother's homecoming. He can't get past the injustice of it all. He's stuck. I think what's at play here is made clear in a little essay Dorothy Sayers wrote back in the '40s:

Envy hates to see other men happy. . . . It begins by asking, plausibly: "Why should I not enjoy what others enjoy?" and it ends by demanding: "Why should others enjoy what I may not?" Envy is the great leveller: if it cannot level things up, it will level them down; and the words constantly in its mouth are "My Rights" and "My Wrongs."[1]

The older son thinks he's been wronged. He's envious and offended. He's comparing his life to his brother's, and everything turns ugly from there. We never get his name; it might be Offended Justice, or What About Me? Whatever it is, he's the forerunner of social media.

Did you know there's a direct link between the rise of envy, depression, and one's use of social media? So much research is coming out on this; let's read from a review of six studies summarized in *Forbes*:

Part of the reason Facebook makes people feel socially isolated (even though they may not actually be) is the comparison factor. We fall into the trap of comparing ourselves to others as we scroll through our feeds, and make judgements about how we measure up. One study looked at how we make comparisons to others posts, in "upward" or "downward" directions—that is, feeling that we're either better or worse off than our friends. It turned out that both types of comparisons made people feel worse, which is surprising, since in real life, only upward comparisons (feeling another person has it better than you) makes people feel bad. But in the social network world, it seems that any kind of comparison is linked to depressive symptoms. . . .

It's no secret that the comparison factor in social media leads to jealousy—most people will admit that seeing other people's tropical vacations and perfectly behaved kids is envy-inducing. Studies have certainly shown that social media use triggers feelings of jealousy. The authors of one study, looking at jealousy and other negative feelings while using Facebook, wrote that "This magnitude of envy incidents taking place on FB alone is astounding, providing evidence that FB offers a breeding ground for invidious feelings." They add that it can become a vicious cycle: feeling jealous can make a person want to make his or her own life look better, and post jealousy-inducing posts of their own, in an endless circle of one-upping and feeling jealous.[2]

It seems there's a good bit of the older brother in all of us. This stuff is thousands of years old, it's just that the Internet has given it an unprecedented platform, and it's exploding.

Then came along *Time*'s cover story, "Why We're Losing the Internet to the Culture of Hate."[3] There are the trolls, of course, but their poisonous hatred is not all that's going on. The internet—especially social media, marketing, and politics—is filled with envy and offense. Our politics have nothing to do with the common good; it's currently ruled by self interest and "special interest groups." In order to become an influence, you need to stir envy, offense, and anger in your followers; it's all about who can you get mad enough to join your side against all the other guys. The recent presidential elections are a case in point: "They're doing this to our country— aren't you offended!?"

Envy first brings depression: "My life isn't as good as yours." Then comes offense: "Why should you have what I don't have?" Which degrades into hatred. Our culture is characterized by the Offended Self.

> Psychologists call this the online disinhibition effect, in which factors like anonymity, invisibility, a lack of authority and not communicating in real time strip away the mores society spent millennia building. And it's seeping from our smartphones into every aspect of our lives.[4]

If I were writing a book on what has gone wrong in culture and politics, I would call it *The Triumph of the Offended Self.* That's the banner flying over our moment in history.

GENTLY, NOW

This is not a sociological critique. We have far higher aims than that. We are here to make room in our souls for the God we love, clearing out debris, experiencing so much more of him. Notice that the older brother can't receive the father's generosity; he's closed off, curtained off, by his attention to Self. This is the hidden danger I spoke of: the stubborn life of the Self. The Exalted Me, unsubmitted and unsurrendered to the rule of Christ in me.

Coming home from that business trip I didn't want to take, exhausted, "hangry," just wanting to be in my own bed, my frustrations were further compounded by a cancelled flight. I queued up at the ticket counter with hundreds of angry travelers, hoping to grab the few available seats on the last outbound jet. I was almost to the counter, which enabled me to see the countenance of the young agent trying her best to help the belligerent man in front of me. He was top drawer in their frequent flyer program and had seven reasons to demand one of the coveted seats. I was rehearsing that exact same speech when I saw the weariness in her eyes. It stopped me; Jesus rescued me from adding to it. For the Self cares nothing about a ticket agent and the terrible day she's had. It is all about my rights and my wrongs.

Over time, throughout our lives, the Self stakes out its own territory within us to assure getting its own way, ordering our world to its likings. It has imbedded assumptions and privileges in our psyche; there is a momentum to its desires, motives, and presence in us. I call this the Self Life.

It's the Self Life in us that so easily takes offense, *enjoys* taking offense.

It wants things done our way, so it's continually making demands, because, of course, our demands are perfectly reasonable, justified. The Self Life doesn't like being interrupted, cut off on the freeway, told what to do or *how* to do things; it hates when someone corrects our driving, typing, cooking, performance (or writing). It's the Self Life in us that keeps a record of wrongs, holds those imaginary conversations with people we'd love to set straight, crafts those devastating emails we only wish we could send. (The anonymity of the Internet lets the Self say anything with impunity; thus, the trolls.)

This isn't a matter of Christian and non-Christian; the Self Life has a religious version. It gets irritated when a prayer time goes longer than we think it should, it feels wronged when church services run late, and it doesn't particularly enjoy worship. The Self waits to be asked during small group how *we* are doing, and it feels righteously irritated when someone else takes too long talking about their life. The Self Life hasn't given a thought about the return of Christ, because it's totally focused on the here and now—making things work out *now*—and it's quietly angry when people suggest our hopes should to be set on the life to come.

Are you beginning to recognize the Self Life? In you?

One of the great embarrassments of Christianity, something that distresses Christians and non-Christians alike, is the fact that people who have aligned themselves with Jesus Christ can still act in such vain, stupid, pompous, mean, and hateful ways. The simple explanation is, they've continued to operate from the Self Life. So when someone crosses them in some way, thwarts their politics, theology, personal ambitions, they feel no qualms about character assassination because their offended Self is at the helm. This also explains the great moral scandals in Christian leadership: There was a hold-out of the Self Life in them. Somewhere along the way, that Self said, *It's time for something for me; I deserve to have this*, and they have an affair, or embezzle funds, or far kinkier stuff. Some of these leaders may have been serving all those years out of genuine union with Christ, but a big part of their act was actually fueled by the Self Life, and it eventually took them down.

In fact, I have a public apology to make. Unfortunately, I can't remember the name of the person to whom I should be making it.

Years ago some kind soul sent me a book on the devil. It was rather dated, from the 1960s I believe, complete with little caricature drawings of Satan as our adversary. I'm ashamed to admit my first thought was, *I know plenty about spiritual warfare; this looks juvenile.* I was put off by the outdated style and comic drawings of the devil as a horned figure, something from Halloween. I'm very grateful to say that just as I was getting ready to toss it out, Jesus said to me, *There's something in here for you.* So I opened the book and began to read.

The author was making a claim that our enemy has a secret hold in each one of us, an access point from within. That got my attention; we'd been dealing with a great deal of spiritual attack, and I was eager for new tools that would gain us a more lasting victory. The author went on to say that this trap door, this inside access the devil has in every person is the Self. Part of me knew it was true, so I read on.

Satan's fall was brought about because he chose to exalt himself over God:

How you are fallen from heaven,

O shining star, son of the morning!

You have been thrown down to the earth,

you who destroyed the nations of the world.

For you said to yourself,

"I will ascend to heaven and set my throne above God's

stars. . . .

I will climb to the highest heavens

and be like the Most High." (Isaiah 14:12–14 NLT)

Later, he found in mankind something of the same weakness, stubbornness, and self-centeredness, that he successfully leveraged to have us follow his lead: we chose to disobey God and reach for what we want, and so we exalted ourselves over our Creator Father. We replaced God with Self on the throne of our life. The author of the little book I was sent went on to explain that the devil doesn't particularly care what your personal sins are, how he gets you to stumble; what he delights in is this internal access he has, the precious Self. For while we entertain the Self, pamper it, let it have its way, we crowd out the life of God. (Remember the older brother standing outside the party, blind to his Father's love.)

That struck me, stayed with me, and over the years has proven to be enormously helpful.

So I'd like to make my apology here and now for not being grateful, and for my arrogant posture toward the gift. (The irony, of course—you saw this coming—is that it was the Self in me that didn't like the gift. My disdain was the illustration for the very truth of it.)

ENORMOUS RELIEF

Now, talking about the Self Life is a difficult thing to do, because there are teachings that sound very righteous and holy, which basically say that anything connected to your humanity is the Self Life and must be crucified. Any desire, any dream, even your own gifting is something essentially contaminated and needs to be killed to get on with your Christian life. I've seen this interpretation cripple many earnest followers of Jesus, and I've seen it turn away many possible seekers. That is *not* how God feels about your humanity.

Why would your Father say things like he will give you the desires of your heart, and please protect your heart because it is the spring of life in you, if what he wanted you to do was kill your desires and dreams?[5] In the chapter on kindness we saw that Jesus never said we're supposed to hate ourselves, for how can we love our neighbor as ourselves if we hate ourselves? (The way you treat your heart is the way you will treat everyone else's.) Jesus always handled broken and misguided people graciously and with a view toward their restoration. The Incarnation itself ought to remove every doubt that God loves and cherishes your humanity, because he took on humanity himself in order to redeem yours. Your personhood is not the problem; the issue is who is at the helm? What is fueling and motivating your faculties? Who gets to drive the bus?

When we let Self rule, it obscures our awareness of God, thwarts our ability to receive him. And the Self Life is a crushing burden to bear.

For the Self was never meant to be master, and when we make it so, we fall prey to a thousand heartaches. Countless pressures, to begin with, because life is now up to us; we are masters of our own destiny, and that's a crushing load. Fear and anxiety soon follow, because we're on our own and we know we can't control the future, not even the next five minutes. The soul shakes and collapses under the weight of it all. We harbor unforgiveness, resentment, and injured pride, because we just can't let go of our memories of injustices we've suffered. My rights, my wrongs. Benevolent detachment is nearly impossible for the exalted Self; it's way too caught up in all the drama. Anger and rage are the usual reactions of the thwarted Self, because we're being denied. Depression often results when the Self is continually thwarted. (Not all depression, of course; it has emotional and neurochemical sources as well, so don't hear me lumping it all in under Self.)

Finally come various forms of self-hatred: self-contempt, rejection, shame. Because the Self is bound to disappoint: it falls short, it fails to reach our ideal view of ourselves, it causes us to do things we later regret, and we end up under the clouds of self-hatred.

The Self is a mighty poor savior and an utterly empty god.

Which is why being rid of the exalted Self is such a glorious relief.

"Now, the self can be regarded in two ways," wrote Lewis. "On the one hand, it is God's creature, an occasion of love and rejoicing; now, indeed, hateful in condition, but to be pitied and healed." Pause there for a moment, and let that sink in—pitied and healed. Not hated. Lewis continued, "On the other hand, it is that one self of all others which is called *I* and *me*, and which on that ground puts forward an irrational claim to preference [like angry passengers in the ticket line, myself included]. This claim is to be not only hated, but simply killed."[6]

Which is why Jesus said we must crucify the rule of Self in us. Often.

What that looks like is something that needs explaining.

WHAT WE DO WITH THE SELF

Some of you Narnia fans might remember the sneering little brat Eustace, who shows up in *The Voyage of the Dawn Treader*. He is insufferable, because he can only ever see the world through the lens of his offended Self. Eustace always feels cheated, wronged—given the smallest portions, the hardest chores—denied his rights at every turn. Shirking those chores one day, he stumbles upon a dragon's treasure and covets it with all his tiny, self-centered heart. His envy, pride, offense, and greed swell to dragon-size, and the little tyrant becomes a dragon himself (illustrating the idea that the Self Life is what gives our enemy access within us). At first he loves the thought of finally being able to "get even" with all the people he believes have been unfair to him. But being a dragon, when you are meant to be a boy, is a very sad life, and Eustace weeps bitter tears over his condition:

> He wanted to get back among humans and talk and laugh and share things. He realised that he was a monster cut off from the whole human race. An appalling loneliness came over him. He began to see that the others had not really been fiends at all. He began to wonder if he himself had been such a nice person as he had always supposed. He longed for their voices. He would have been grateful for a kind word even from Reepicheep [a character Eustace thoroughly disliked].
>
> When he thought of this the poor dragon that had been Eustace lifted up its voice and wept. A powerful dragon crying its eyes out under the moon in a deserted valley is a sight and a sound hardly to be imagined.[7]

These are probably the first healthy feelings Eustace ever had. He needs to be "un-dragoned," but no matter how much he claws at his own scales, he can't get rid of his dragon-ness. Only the great lion, Aslan, can do it for him, and it hurt, and it was wonderful:

> I was afraid of his claws, I can tell you, but I was pretty nearly desperate now. So I just lay flat down on my back to let him do it.
>
> The very first tear he made was so deep that I thought it had gone right into my heart. And when he began pulling the skin

off, it hurt worse than anything I've ever felt. The only thing that made me able to bear it was just the pleasure of feeling the stuff peel off. You know—if you've ever picked the scab of a sore place. It hurts like billy-oh but it is such fun to see it coming away. . . .

Well, he peeled the beastly stuff right off—just as I thought I'd done it myself the other three times, only they hadn't hurt—and there it was lying on the grass: only ever so much thicker, and darker, and more knobbly looking than the others had been. And there was I as smooth and soft as a peeled switch and smaller than I had been. Then he caught hold of me—I didn't like that much for I was very tender underneath now that I'd no skin on—and threw me into the water. It smarted like anything but only for a moment. After that it became perfectly delicious and as soon as I started swimming and splashing I found that all the pain had gone from my arm. And then I saw why. I'd turned into a boy again.[8]

Anyone delivered from the offended Self knows this exquisite relief.

Which is why Jesus said we must take up our cross and die to the supremacy of Self every single day, probably many times a day (Matthew 10:38; 16:24; Mark 8:34; Luke 9:23; 14:27). He *wants* us to experience this exquisite relief; why else did he come? Even just this morning, I woke with the Self and its demands far more present to me than I felt present to God. Of course, God is right here, but the Self is a curtain pulled between us. So I needed to begin my day with a simple prayer: *I give the Self Life to you, God. I abandon it, release it, deny it, turn it over to you. I'd much rather have you.*

We must crucify the exalted, offended Self, that's clear. But what this looks like in operation has left many dear folks a little confused. Let's hear from George MacDonald again:

> It is not to thwart or tease the poor self, Jesus tells us. That was not the purpose for which God gave it to us. He tells us we must leave it altogether—yield it, deny it, refuse it, lose it: thus only shall we save it, thus only have a share in our own being. The self is given to us that we may sacrifice it; it is ours that we like Christ may have [something] to offer—not that we should torment it, but that we should deny it . . . refuse, abandon, deny altogether self as a ruling, or determining, or originating element in us.[9]

In other words, the simple thing I do (I'm trying to practice this every day) is to pray, *Jesus, I surrender the Self Life to you.* I'm not hating the Self; I'm not mocking it. I'm not berating the Self, not heaping accusation and contempt upon it. I am surrendering it, turning it over to Jesus, relinquishing its every right. Here are some practical ways:

"Envy cannot bear to admire or respect. It cannot bear to be grateful," wrote Sayers.[10] So a wonderful way to thwart the Self is to *admire and be grateful.* Pray for people who are in a better situation than you are, who are more gifted than you are, or who currently have wonderful circumstances coming their way. Rejoice with those who rejoice. Pray for someone else's promotion, someone else's pregnancy, someone else's healing. That crucifies envy.

Make no room for offense. Given the social air we breathe, this is going to be *enormously* helpful. Whenever, wherever you see offense cropping up, crucify it—give it no hold. Now, I understand it may be utterly justified. People do offensive things; all those Eustaces out there *are* offensive. Cutting in on you at the market, taking your place in the theater, getting on social media and saying all kinds of terrible things. But the point is, you don't want to get caught up in it. Offense has no good ending.

This morning I had a little victory. I was checking email before working, and somebody had sent me the most offensive email. The rampant Self out there feels perfectly entitled to correct others, critique, post negative reviews. But this was so baseless, and I had such a delicious reply. I was ready to send off a devastating two-sentence rebuke when Jesus said, *Why? Don't even entertain offense. Let it go, John; just hit Delete. You don't want to give ground to that.*

Cultivate admiration. When you're scrolling through social media (which I hope is less and less these days), and you come across someone's wonderful life, cheer for them. Praise God for it. Make it personal: "Lord, she's such a wonderful singer; I pray she gets chosen to lead worship next week instead of me." "Jesus, he's such a fabulous athlete; I pray he makes the team." Goodbye, Self. You cannot have my soul.

Oh, the joy of it—the enormous relief. I would rather have so much more of God than coddle the little tyrant of Self. And as soon as I crucify the Self, God is right there, and now there's so much more room in me for him to fill.

By the way—this is why the Christian life only works through total abandonment. You have to be all in. If we hold anything back, retain some part of our lives for ourselves, large or small, the Self will rule there and continually set itself against God in us. A house divided cannot stand. Most disappointing Christian experiences can be explained by the honest admission that they weren't abandoned to God. There's no other way to follow Christ; with utter, brilliant clarity he said it this way: "Whoever tries to keep their life will lose it, and whoever loses their life will preserve it" (Luke 17:33).

GIVING IT A TRY

However you want to describe it, you turn over the Self Life every morning. Deny it, abandon it, ignore it. Let God be your God; let Jesus be your operational Lord. Take up your cross daily. It's an utter relief.

Free yourself from the culture of comparison, envy, and the offended Self by unplugging from the matrix of the internet whenever possible. Why swim in that stuff?

Pray for other people's success—this really puts down the Self Life in us.

When talking with someone, don't secretly wait your turn. Be present to them; let the focus remain on them until they ask about you. Even if they never do.

Worship. Really. Make a regular practice of putting on some worship music and lifting up Jesus.

And for the purposes of finding God, as we turn over the Self to him, we also ask for more of God. Pull back the curtain of Self, and God is right there.

The relief will astonish you.

ten

CARING FOR NEGLECTED

PLACES IN YOUR SOUL

Last spring my dear wife left town for seven days. She was in great need of some personal time away, soul care, time alone with God. Which left me at home with the dogs, horses, normal household chores, and my work. *And . . .* an empty house, with evenings to do whatever I wanted. I pictured myself in all sorts of masculine bachelor rhapsody: hours of cable television, watching premier soccer and hunting shows; cereal for dinner; dressing from laundry still in heaps on the couch.

After I got home from dropping Stasi off at the airport, I kicked off my shoes and looked around, wondering which of the personal joys to begin with. That's when God stepped in. *Get out your journal,* he said. Now, to be fair, getting some time with God was on my agenda too. Absolutely. I just didn't have it taking place quite so suddenly. Maybe after that pastrami sandwich and the second half of the Liverpool game. I stood in the middle of the living room, a man vacillating between clarity and denial. Maybe I hadn't heard a thing.

Get out your journal, Jesus repeated. *You have neglected your soul.*

A long sigh. That I knew—my soul *felt* neglected. I slowly walked to my office to retrieve my journal and returned to the living room where I sat down: the guilty schoolboy who knows he's been slouching on his assignments, is not too happy to be found out, and is repentant enough to sit ready with pen in hand, wondering where the Master was going next.

"Where have I neglected my soul, Lord?" I asked.

In your ungrieved griefs, he replied.

Another sigh. My, he was moving quickly. Oh, I knew he was right. I mean, this wasn't anywhere on my radar, but once Jesus named it, I knew it was the missing thing—the overlooked and unattended place. (Sometimes it takes someone else to name the thing right in front of us that we cannot see.) Soccer and hunting shows were not going to address my real needs.

So I began to write out a list of losses and disappointments from the past eighteen months. It wasn't at all heavy or dark; it was cathartic. The relief in simply naming things was palpable. For the grief, or disappointment, or sadness is in there, recognized or not, and it takes a lot of energy to keep it below the surface. Letting it rise, naming its sources, is relieving. That beach ball we've been trying to hold underwater gets to pop up, and we don't have to suppress it anymore.

AVOIDANCE

Our son's childhood bedroom was in the basement, directly beneath the upstairs bathroom. When you flushed the toilet or drained the bath, it sounded like water was running down through the walls. Almost like a Disney attraction. One day I noticed that the toilet upstairs had gone quite loose on its setting, and it made me nervous. *How long has it been like that?* I immediately went downstairs to the bedroom and looked up at the ceiling . . . sure enough, there was a small but noticeable water stain. *Gadzooks.*

I fetched a ladder from the garage, along with a small tool for cutting drywall, and proceeded to test the ceiling for how far the damage had gone. I was expecting the worst (we always fear the worst) and wouldn't have been surprised if, after a little poking around, a three foot square of ceiling dropped out, toilet and plumbing with it. Much to my relief, the water leak appeared to be intermittent (the drywall was not soaked, only stained), and I knew the next step was to replace the section of ceiling and reseat the toilet with a new gasket and bolts. But I postponed doing so.

For one year.

That's right—an entire year. It slipped my mind. To be fair, I really did forget; to be *honest*, I was in denial. I didn't want to take on that project, so it was easy to let it "slip from my mind."

It's human nature to want our problems to simply go away. Be honest now—how many of us have heard a troubling *tick, tick, tick* or *thump, thump, thump* coming from the general direction of our car's engine or transmission and not done a thing about it, hoping it would just go away? We do this with our health all the time—that painful little hitch, the lump, the troubling indigestion, those few extra pounds cry for our attention, but we let it pass for months or even years, hoping it will magically sort itself out.

How much more our souls. In this busy, mad, distracted world, it's just too easy (and far more efficient) to send your soul to the back of the bus. Low priority. Maybe later. But you, my reader, have read this far, and I'm so proud of you! You're making the hard choices that will bear fruit for years and years to come.

So . . . next step. Let's talk about neglected places in your soul.

I'm beginning the conversation with neglected loss, disappointment, and grief not because these are the main issues in any person's life, but because these are the things we tend to run from. Of course we do. We run from pain, run back to our normal lives, try to pretend we aren't bereaved, bereft, whatever the loss may be. Problem is, we are running from huge tracts of our own soul, leaving them behind, and then we can't find more of God because we are looking with so little of our own soul.

It takes more of *you* to find more of God.

That's a big idea, so let me explain. My first dog was a Great Pyrenees–Border Collie mix, a big smart dog that looked like a wolf and played like a puppy. His name was Joshua. Never once in his life was he on a leash. He was the best dog I ever had, and when I lost him, I didn't know if I ever wanted another.

Years later we got Scout, our first family dog, a big male Golden

Retriever who loved hiking, canoeing, and underwear. He was a great dog; losing him was heartbreaking, and I found myself giving less of my heart to our next Golden, Oban, who we lost this fall. Now we have a female Golden named Maisie, and I'm aware she has even less of me. Over time, each loss causes us to offer less and less next time. What's available in us is lessened through our losses.

We often can't find the more of God we long for, because we are looking with so little of ourselves. Too much of us has been left behind. Just as the assault on our attention keeps pushing us into the shallows, so we no longer hear deep calling unto deep, the pace of life rushes us past significant moments of disappointment and loss, and in doing so continues the "shallowfication" of our souls. We are like eroded stream banks, a little more shaved off every year. Or like the lonesome hero in "Desperado," who was losing all his "highs and lows" as his feelings simply went away.

So this is a good place to push back. We may have neglected our soul's need for beauty. We may have neglected our soul's need for play. But I have reason to believe that unattended loss is a good place to start if you would recover and heal the vessel God *wants* to fill, if you would open up room in your life for him to meet you there.

HONESTY IS KINDNESS

A friend just lost his job. Another couple can't get pregnant. The son of other friends tried to take his life last month. I mentioned earlier the loss of a young man in our church. Burying our dear family dog. A dear friend of dear friends just had her feet amputated, the result of toxic shock syndrome from a completely unknown cause. The young wife of a friend doesn't want to have sex with her husband; she was abused as a child, and while my friend completely understands, it's pretty rough on a marriage not to share physical intimacy for decades. The clerk at the grocers told me yesterday he gave up being a Christian; you know he has his reasons. So let's just make this clear—we live in a brutal world. Do I really need to convince anyone of this?

A world like this damages your soul as a matter of daily business. We must live wisely in return.

A colleague was reeling under the news of the loss of a childhood playmate. "Give yourself three months," I said. This is my standard line for grief. Not because it's a magic number, but because it's long enough to be realistic and short enough that people just might listen. No one enjoys hanging around grief. We want it to go away as quickly as possible, like an alcoholic uncle who chain-smokes in your house and makes loud, inappropriate comments, and all you want is for him to leave. The madness about grief is you think you'll feel better in a few days. Certainly in a few weeks. The average bereavement leave in corporate America is four days for a spouse or child and three days for a parent.[1] Three days. That's complete insanity. It communicates an illusion that's totally detached from reality. At three days you haven't even begun to breathe. At four days you are still in total concussive shock. So I suggest three months of margin and soul care to someone in grief, because it shatters that illusion and suggests an open space of time where real grieving and healing can begin. *Begin.* Because who knows how long it really will take.

This cannibalistic world isn't going to say this to you, sure isn't going to act like it, so allow me to say it: your losses matter.

Oh, what kindness we begin to practice when we act like our losses matter.

This is why part of my soul-care regimen now includes a baseball bat and plastic trash bin. Our neighborhood requires the bins provided by the trash company; they are large, awkward, and nearly indestructible. Which make them perfect for hammering on with a baseball bat. Loss, disappointment, grief, and injustice provoke anger, and you've got to have somewhere to take it. (As a therapist, I've found suppressed anger morphs into fear, which is no better.) I like to go out and give my bin a good thrashing when I'm in touch with the hurt and anger, the thievery and loss. (I do recommend closing the garage door if you can; you might alarm the neighbors.) We must do something with our rage. And let me add—of course you're angry. Your rage is not a sign that something's wrong with you; there's something wrong with the world. In some ways, everything is wrong with the world. We're often embarrassed by our anger, but it's simply proof that our hearts are aching for things to be *right*.

AS YOU BEGIN TO ALLOW
YOUR LOSSES TO MATTER

So—Stasi left for seven days, and Jesus seized the moment to take me into my losses, because I'd treated them like the leaky bathroom—with total neglect. He invited me first to name them and then, one by one, invite his healing love into these places. Some were great—the loss of a dear friend to cancer—and some were small. My intended week of frat house bingeing turned into something so much more kind and healing.

As Mark Twain said, it takes years before you know the extent of your loss:

> A man's house burns down. The smoking wreckage represents only a ruined home that was dear through years of use and pleasant associations. By and by, as the days and weeks go on, first he misses this, then that, then the other thing. And, when he casts about for it, he finds that it was in that house. Always it is an essential—there was but one of its kind. It cannot be replaced. It was in that house. It is irrevocably lost. He did not realize that it was an essential when he had it; he only discovers it now when he finds himself balked, hampered, by its absence. It will be years before the tale of lost essentials is complete, and not till then can he truly know the magnitude of his disaster.[2]

There is the initial loss, but as time goes by there are all the other losses: no one to call when you want to talk about that thing the two of you used to talk about, no one to share the joy when your favorite team wins. There's just an emptiness in your life now. I had grieved the initial loss, but what I was totally ignoring were all the other things lost in the burning down of that house.

I also paid attention to the process, began to take note of what helped me during that week and what hurt. Now, I realize that in my tenderness I was in a heightened state of sensitivity, but I found it revealing for that very reason—I could tell immediately what helped my dear soul, what did not, and what was bordering harmful. It was an epiphany; half the stuff we do to ourselves on a daily basis is actually pretty hurtful.

Television hurt. Even though I usually enjoy vegging out over my shows, I couldn't do TV. It was abrasive, like someone shouting at you when you've just broken an eardrum. Isn't that fascinating? It simply didn't feel nourishing. I mentioned earlier the research indicating that simply watching traumatic events can be traumatizing to the soul—and if you consume any TV at all, you've seen thousands of traumatic events. A therapist colleague told me that when he began his clinical work helping Vietnam veterans, he started having his own flashbacks—even though he was never in Nam. "I had nightmares of men dying; I would flinch when a car backfired. Their stories were so devastating, my soul was having sympathetic trauma reactions." Something research is proving true for many caregivers.[3]

I tried watching *Gladiator*. Normally, I love that movie. When I turned the channel on, the scene unfolding happened to be one of the big coliseum battle scenes. Part of me was drawn into the moment; a deeper part of my soul cringed; I had to turn it off. Hmmm . . . it made me wonder what I normally subject my soul to.

I needed to give up stimulants. Nicotine, caffeine, sugar—all those things we use to prop up our daily happiness will, over time, burn out the soul. Because the soul can't always be "on." (I was in one of those gas station quick marts the other day, and I was shocked at the size of the cooler devoted to energy drinks. It used to just be Red Bull and a few others; now there are dozens and dozens, floor to ceiling. They take up more space than water. We are forcing our souls into a perpetual state of anxiety, and that is super damaging, like redlining your car's RPMs all the time.) The pace of life, lack of any transitions, and state of always being plugged into our phones and technology reduces our living to one continuous experience of being "on." That'll wipe you out for sure. The world does enough to fry your soul; you certainly don't want to add to it through overstimulation.

By contrast, the "graces" in this book are designed to help your soul come down from hypervigilant mode, or constant distraction, or the dopamine "loop"—whatever you are caught in. This allows your body, brain, and soul to calm down, to find Christ again.

> Creating sensations that say there is no emergency helps calm the body's alert system (hypothalamic-pituitary-adrenal or HPA system) so the brain (prefrontal cortex) can regain its ability to think and plan. Allowing yourself to experience the uncomfortable

emotions (without feeding them and making them more intense) enables the emotions to pass. Soothing yourself helps you tolerate the experience without acting in ways that are not helpful in the long run, or blocking the emotions, which makes the emotions grow larger or come out in ways you didn't intend.[4]

There's an enormous difference between relief and restoration, as I said; much of what provided me relief in the past was not helping heal these neglected places I was intentionally surfacing. Allow me a brief list . . .

Helpful: Generous amounts of sunshine. Everything living and green. Long walks. Lonesome country roads. Swimming. Beauty. Music. Water. Friendly dogs. (I've never understood it when someone says to me, "Yeah—we're not really dog people." That's like saying, "Yeah—we're not really happiness people.") Compassion. Not expecting myself to produce the same level of work I normally accomplish in a day. Yard work. Building a fence.

Unhelpful: Grocery stores. Malls. Television. Traffic. Draining people wanting to talk to me. (Friends and family are at this moment wondering if they fall into this category. It's reserved for people who live out of touch with their own soul—and thus mine. "The way you treat your own heart.") Airports. The news—especially politics. Social media. Your typical dose of movie violence.

Now, which cluster of the things I've just named above make up most of your weekly routine? Do you begin to see more clearly how essential it is that we intentionally care for our neglected heart and soul?

My friends, I really don't want to be the unwelcome prophet, but the fact is this: life is not going to get better on this planet. It's going to get worse before it gets better; all signs indicate it's getting worse at an alarming rate. "If you have raced with men on foot and they have worn you out, how can you compete with horses? If you stumble in safe country, how will you manage in the thickets by the Jordan?" (Jeremiah 12:5). In other words, if you think this is hard, wait'll you see what's coming next. We're going to want our souls strong and ready for the days ahead, filled with God, not fried and empty. So we must practice soul care.

GIVING IT A TRY

I'm not suggesting you go on a witch hunt for every neglected place in your soul. There's way too much loss in there to take on all at once. Many people are afraid to feel any of it, fearing that if they start crying, they'll never stop. It isn't true, but let's be kind; let's approach this realistically. Pick one thing you would call a loss or disappointment that you feel you've had to put aside because there wasn't time or space to deal with it when it happened. (This is partly why I loved *H is for Hawk*—Macdonald had lost her father, and it was her life with a young hawk and the woods that allow her grief room to come up and be healed.)

You don't have to give a week to this (unless you have a week to give, and Jesus seizes it for that purpose). Just begin to name your losses; write them down. What was lost—a friendship, a hope, an opportunity that might have shaped your future? It's so important to name it. (When I say "put some words to it," I mean out loud. Say to the room around you what you are uncovering, how that discovery makes you feel. Better still, I encourage you to write it down.)

Has a movie or song brought you to tears recently (perhaps there's a song that always brings a few tears?). Play it again, and pay attention—why? What is this awakening in you? Put some words to it. The neglected losses are in there; give them a voice.

Then what? Allow your soul to *feel*. Don't tell it what to feel; it knows what to do. Just give it permission. It might be anger at first, or it might be sadness, loneliness, *why bother?* You might find yourself shouting some profanities—*that's okay*. Your losses matter. Don't edit yourself into silence.

Anger is a pretty common first reaction to unattended loss. Let it out. Grab a kitchen spatula and start whacking the pillows on your couch, all the while naming why you are so angry over this loss. You might try the baseball bat and trash bin, but do be careful with your first couple of swings. My bin is quite resilient and sends the bat bouncing right back at me. You want to get some practice at this before you really let it fly. But oh, how good it is to let it fly.

What you're doing through this practice is becoming present to your own soul, to places that were left behind.

The next step is to invite Jesus in. Invite his love, his comfort, his presence into this specific loss, for his presence brings mercy and healing. I find it important to ask, "What do you have to say about this, God? What are you saying to me about my losses?" His comforting words of interpretation, or promise, are part of the healing.

Sometimes what I need is a walk to my little stream. I just need to sit, and sitting by water really helps. Beauty heals; beauty contains within it the promise of restoration.

I haven't had a chance to describe this elsewhere, so let me explain a dynamic in how God heals the soul; it fits perfectly here. In the past, when I became aware of something in my soul needing his touch, mercy, or deep healing, I would bring it to Jesus in prayer and ask him to do so. The results were mixed. Sometimes it seemed to work, sometimes not. During my road trip to Montana, Jesus began to show me something quite helpful—we can't stand at a distance from our own soul and ask Christ to "go in there and deal with it." This isn't hostage negotiation; we don't hide a block away and hope God takes care of business. This is your own soul we're talking about; the door opens from the inside. "I stand at the door and knock," Jesus explained. "If anyone hears my voice and opens the door, I will come in" (Revelation 3:20). We open the door to our soul *from the inside*. This is the purpose of naming the loss, feeling it, allowing ourselves to return to the place in our own being that we walked away from. We must enter these places ourselves—the memory, the emotion, whatever it is we are aware of. We *inhabit* our own soul again. Jesus insists on it. Once there, we open the door from the inside, inviting Christ in, which he is always so eager to do.

Your soul is a beautiful instrument, like a cello or piano, capable of a vast range of expression and experience. Over time, strings get broken, keys are lost. Thirty years of this, and there isn't much of us left with which to make music. Though we want God, he is forced to play one or two notes; it's all he has to work with. By attending to the neglected places of our souls, we recover the lost strings and damaged keys. The more we do, the more rich and colorful our life becomes, because God has so much more to make music with.

ASK FOR IT!

Lest we overlook the obvious, let me take a moment's pause here to suggest that in your search for more of God, do remember to ask for it.

Such a simple thought, but so helpful. Sometimes we get so caught up in the process we forget to ask. We have not because we ask not (James 4:2). Ask and you shall receive—that's the promise (Matthew 7:7).

So throughout my day, and over the course of a week, I will pray for the very thing I need most:

> *Father, Jesus, Holy Spirit—I need more of you, God. I need*
> *so much more of you. My soul cries out for you. O Father,*
> *Jesus, Holy Spirit—fill me with more of you, God. I need more*
> *of you; I pray for so much more of you. Saturate me.*

eleven

THE GIFTS OF MEMORY

It's deep winter now in Colorado. Our grass has not been green for months—I hardly remember running barefoot through it. We got six inches of snow last night, and I'm not frolicking in that; I'm indoors slogging through email, online banking, and airline reservations for some business travel I really don't want to commit to. Well, I was until I paused, picked up a river stone from my desk, and wandered back to summer and Wyoming.

The stone has a lovely cool feel; it's smooth, glacially polished, and settles perfectly into the palm of my hand. I plucked it out of a creek the last day of our family Teton trip back in the summer, because I knew I'd need it through the long winter. I pause, turning it over in my hands, reaching for a practice that's somewhat new to me—the intentional use of memory to restore my soul and bring me back to God.

I'm drifting now, floating away from email; I'm slipping down the Snake River in a canoe . . .

The river changed so much this year. Some of the old, familiar gravel bars were completely washed away, and there were dozens of new "screens"—deadwood tangles ten to twenty feet high. I counted more than a hundred fresh giant spruces swept downriver, scattered here and there like pick-up sticks. It takes a lot of water and force to pull up spruces and carry them off like driftwood. Apparently, there was a massive runoff last spring, and it left its mark on the river channel. Changes the newcomer would never notice, wouldn't care to notice. But we did and talked about each one, because we've been floating this river for almost twenty years.

We started coming here for vacations back in the '90s. We'd camp or stay in a cabin, canoe, hike, swim, rock jump, look for huckle-berries and wildlife. What began as a search for adventure became something else—an annual pilgrimage, a liturgy of beauty and care-free immersion. You can tell who's been to Ash Wednesday services by the smudge on their brow; you can see our faithful observance to this wilderness ritual on the stern of our canoe, where eighteen old and fading permit stickers create a testimony, like a tattoo.

When you invest yourself in a place over time, every return grows richer, because you open up a geographical journal of stories, your stories. We put in at Pacific Creek that morning and laughed again over the time McConnell took an overloaded canoe, turned it sideways in the current, swamped, and wrapped it around one of those screens. Thirty seconds after launching.

Even in my memory, I can hear the lap-lapping of the river on the canoe; the glacial silt in the water makes a sandy sound on our hull.

A bald eagle flies overhead. We pass the place we encountered buffalo coming down for a drink. Stop and jump in where we always stop and jump in. Then comes the section where my father's ashes were scattered in the Snake, a river that flows through the ranch town he was raised in, miles from here. We don't say anything—not because we're melancholy, but because nothing needs to be said. We paddle on.

Each year we return lays down a new layer of story and adventure, beauty and encounter. Layer upon layer, like a rich patina on a piece of heirloom furniture, or better, like the technique Rembrandt and the Old Masters used in their painting: carefully laying down dozens of layers of paint to achieve that extraordinary effect of depth and gravitas. The power of building memories, storing them up like good scotch cellared away for winter.

Drifting back now in my mind, I'm reminded how good God is. This stone in my hands is bringing me back to the God I love.

A UNIQUE GIFT

Human beings are remarkable creatures, endowed with extraordinary gifts and delicate faculties.

Don't you just love having a sense of humor? I love cracking up; I love watching my friends and family crack up. Meister Ekhart believed we were born from the laughter of the Trinity.[1] How about the sense of smell or taste? Our sense of smell can pick up one trillion different odors![2] Music remains to me an absolute marvel: the ability of the human ear to detect subtle notes, the grace of the soul to write intricate symphonies. Did you know that our capacity for music doesn't reside in one part of our brain but rather draws upon many different regions? Scientists can't figure out why. Such gifts, so many graces come to us through the endowment of our humanity.

The faculty of memory is particularly exquisite. I think there's a secret to why God provided it.

Certainly we can't learn without memory; language requires the retention of sounds, symbols, and their meanings, which build toward a complex framework of speech and reading over time. You couldn't balance your checkbook if you didn't recall simple math; you couldn't hold a job without the ability to recollect myriad specific procedures; and you wouldn't have one single relationship if you didn't remember a person's face, let alone their life. Without memory we couldn't make our way in the world. We'd be lost as toddlers every single day because we couldn't find our way home. I remember as the new kid missing my bus stop the first day of summer school; I was terrified into silence, and only when the entire busload of children had been deposited at each of their well-known stops did the driver look back and find one weepy boy too embarrassed to admit he'd missed his own.

But there's something more, something touchingly merciful about memory. It has to do with a common occurrence of loss so near to us, so constant, that we've grown completely numb to it—or numbed by it: our inability to make time stand still, even for a moment. No sooner have we stepped into some wonderful life experience—a birthday, a wedding, that Christmas morning when you were six years old and the pond had frozen and you got your first pair of skates—but in the next breath it is completely swept away in the unceasing river of time, swept far downstream and out of reach.

Every precious moment will suddenly be last week, last month, last year before you can blink.

I remember (there is memory again) a conversation I had as a therapist with a young mother. She came to see me not because of some crisis, but in tears nevertheless over the passage of her children's childhood right before her eyes. "These are such precious, precious days," she wept, "and they are passing so quickly I can't hang onto them. I can hardly bear it; I'm grieving during days that ought to be joyful." Few of us remember the taste of our first ice cream (what flavor was it?), the first book we read ourselves, our first kiss. We can barely recall that vacation we planned for so many years; it was over in mere weeks.

I name this loss because it *is* loss—tragic, sweeping, and expansive. Your entire life, every dear moment, is currently being swept downstream from you even as you read this sentence. It does such harm to the soul and our life with God. All good things come to an end. I hate that phrase, hate it like the sound of sirens, the sound of dirt falling on a casket.

Lest we despair, God has given us "a future and a hope" (Jeremiah 29:11 NLT) and to be quite specific, it includes the restoration of every precious day of our lives. Heaven is not a memory wipe. It is the time and capacity to truly relish the story of our lives, to see the hand of God in it all (how many times angels rescued you), to be vindicated, and even rewarded.

> "Lord, when did we see you hungry and feed you, or thirsty and give you something to drink? When did we see you a stranger and invite you in, or needing clothes and clothe you? When did we see you sick or in prison and go to visit you?" The King will reply, "Truly I tell you, whatever you did for one of the least of these brothers and sisters of mine, you did for me" (Matthew 25:37–40).

Notice that this promise cannot be fulfilled unless our stories are known, down to the smallest details.

Your story matters. Your story will not be lost. But I wrote more fully about that in a book entitled *All Things New*, so I will only mention it here. All good things do *not* come to an end. Not even close.

In the meantime, God in his mercy has given us a grace for this recurrent, incessant, unavoidable, daily experience of loss, and that gift is memory. Through which—*if* we make use of it—we can go back and drink more deeply, savor, take in the full gift of wonderful moments great and small (for the full gift can never be taken in during the moment).

There are so many reasons I should get back to email, but the better choice right now is to sit and remember the river, the white sand beach, the water so cold that diving deep made the surface feel warm, drying in the summer sun. I sigh (there's the sigh). I remember

God is good. The flower of my soul, which had closed against winter's grey cold, is opening again in the warmth of his goodness.

Teewinot is the memoir of Jack Turner, one of the old guards at Exum Mountain Guides in the Teton valley. It's a beautiful book filled with memories from a lifetime leading climbers through the Teton range, especially up the Grand itself. When you've spent your life mountaineering, you have a lot of stories to tell. Most of his friends have died somewhere in the world's highest places. But the book is beautiful, because it is a memoir of a place, this place, and filled with knowledge of flora and fauna and of native history, with his relationship with a place known as intimately as any lifelong friend or spouse. (We are chasing down the gift of memory, and notice here that if we weren't able to retain our precious stories of a place, it would feel like the loss of a loved one when either the place disappears or we can no longer walk there.)

I would reread that book year after year, in the long winters when I could no longer wander those beautiful peaks and meadows. (Surely you know the joys of rereading a favorite book. It's just as good as returning to a favorite place.) Turner takes the reader through a season of climbing in the park. He tells a wild tale of almost dying himself when he went most of the way up the Grand in the dark, on a fall evening, to retrieve some gear, and a snowstorm swept in without warning. He gets disoriented and nearly lost . . .

I'm not equipped to survive a night out and no one knows where I am, my mind becomes a melee of paranoid images. . . . I obsess about who will find me, who will be called first. Or whether, if the storm continues, I will not be found until spring. . . .

The rock is greasy with half-frozen water. In the summer this section is so easy that we don't belay clients, but on this dark night I am exhausted and off balance and oh so keenly aware that even a short fall here could be deadly.

Then, in the darkness, without thought, my right hand searches the right wall of the chimney, brushing away snow. My fingers sink into a great handhold, a handhold I know as well as I know the difference between hot and cold. Yes.

As I climb on, my fingers find more handholds, each buried under snow, each waiting for me like an old friend, each, I want to say, greeting me. Whoever knows a reef or river or mountain intimately knows, at some point, this feeling. It is among the gifts that flow from returning, again and again, each new return enriching the cycle forever.[3]

It is a wonderful thing to know a reef, river, or mountain intimately. Because you can return there in your memory and visit again those times that were so meaningful to you.

TAKING HOLD OF THE GIFT

My friend Dan has an intimate history with the North Fork of the Blackfoot River in Montana, a river many locals believe to be the one Norman Maclean refers to as his "family river" in *A River Runs Through It*. Dan makes an annual pilgrimage there to camp, fish, and run from bears. (He does *not* like bears.) And when he's back in his work world in the city, languishing through long office meetings, he goes back there in his mind, literally wading upriver, fishing it again. The river—an intimate gift from God—thus becomes for him the source of a thousand more gifts through the practice of memory.

When we forget (and oh, how we forget), our senses can trigger an awakening of remembrance and place, and suddenly we are back as though it were yesterday. Sense-memory is such an exquisite gift from God, especially our sense of smell; the olfactory system is the one most laden with memory. You've experienced this I'm sure—one whiff of cut grass, canned peaches, salt air, or pine bark, and you are back in your dearest places and memories. For me, the sweet, moist, almost tobacco-like blend of cottonwood, willow, and river bottom—riparian ecosystems—will forever mean summer, adventure, wildness, family. As I watch the snow fall outside my window, I return to the stories of this past summer, and my soul is nourished. Comforted. Opened again to the goodness of God.

Try this: name three beautiful truths that came to you last year, moments when you had utter clarity and your soul was practically rescued by it. No? How about this: name three delightful gift experiences from God in the last several months. You see what I mean. Forgetfulness is a spiritual pandemic ravaging humanity, with dangerous and lethal repercussions. This is why God strikes the bells to "remember" so often in the Old and New Testaments:

Only be careful, and watch yourselves closely so that you do not forget the things your eyes have seen or let them fade from your heart as long as you live. (Deuteronomy 4:9)

In that day their strong cities . . . will be like places abandoned to thickets and undergrowth. And all will be desolation. You have forgotten God your Savior; you have not remembered the Rock, your fortress. (Isaiah 17:9–10)

Remember, therefore, what you have received and heard; hold it fast. (Revelation 3:3)

If you've spent any time in a more traditional church, the type that still sing hymns, you might recall stumbling across an odd moment during the second stanza of "Come Thou Fount of Every Blessing": "Here I raise my Ebenezer / Hither by Thy help I've come." The rest of the hymn is now lost to me as I get sidetracked with, *What the blazes is an Ebenezer? Why am I raising one? I don't think I have one. Am I supposed to? Would I recognize one if I saw it?* All the while I'm equally distracted by associations with good old Ebenezer Scrooge, which takes me further off on rabbit trails.

This hymn refers to a story from the Old Testament, to one of those fabulous Lord of the Rings–type battles when it looked like Israel was about to be utterly massacred by a marauding army. But God intervened, and he intervened so mightily that the people of God ran their enemies all the way out of the country and then some.

THE GIFTS OF MEMORY

The prophet Samuel then "took a stone and set it up between Mizpah and Shen. He named it Ebenezer, saying, 'Thus far the LORD has helped us'" (1 Samuel 7:12). The point being, every time an Israelite passed that way again, they would see the stone and remember what God had done, remember how utterly faithful he is.

It does the heart good to remember.

So here at my desk I have a number of Ebenezers. A bear tooth, found high on an unnamed pass on a backpacking trip I don't want to forget. Stones that are precious to me: granite from the top of the Grand Teton; a rock from the top of the thousand-foot "prow" on Kit Carson peak; a little round stone from a failed attempt to climb the north buttress of Mt. Sneffels, and the emergency rappel to get off in a lightning storm. This year there's a new addition—this glacially polished stone I'm holding in my hands right now.

By the way, this intentional use of memory is a cure for one of the soul's most common diseases, that "what have you done for me lately?" posture we fall into toward God. That unattractive attitude of ransomed Israel when they whined, "Sure, you delivered us from slavery; you've miraculously fed us every morning; but what about spring water? Can you do that? What about some meat?" I hate this part of me. Will you come through for my children this time? For this trip? This need? It's embarrassing.

Memory pulls us out by turning back to the goodness of God in our past. It allows us to savor the many gifts he has given. I'm suggesting you establish a practice of it.

GIVING IT A TRY

Where are your stones of remembrance? I bet your home or apartment has some—photos, artwork, driftwood from the beach, an etching from the Louvre. Do you pause and let them take you back? Or have they become so familiar that you don't see them anymore? Maybe you should move things around, perhaps acquire some new "stones."

Here's a redemptive use of your phone—it's a library of memories in photos. Pull out your phone during a break, but instead of checking the news feed, browse your photos, let them take you back into precious moments. Linger there, savor the gift.

Where do you keep all those words that once meant so much to you—the clarity you received on your identity? The quote that felt like your life's motto? The counsel you know will save your life if you follow it? The precious truths you know to be true of God? *Write this stuff down!* Put it in little notes to yourself round the house. I'll stick notes on my bathroom mirror: "You are deeply loved." "God is good." Things like that.

This grace requires a little more intentionality than most. The frost appears on the windowpane in front of you, and so you are reminded to let beauty into your soul. Your "pause" reminder helps you practice it through the day (you have set reminders, haven't you?!) Sometimes something will prompt a memory, and if you are able in the moment, go with it, linger, and receive. I've found that I must be more intentional with this grace, and choose to make room for it in my week. But it is always, always worth it.

twelve

BELIEVE

I had an old desk lamp with a wiggly switch, picked up for spare change at a garage sale. It had this annoying habit of turning on and off without rhyme or reason. One moment the room would be lit; next moment I'd be sitting in total darkness. Now this old lamp was cunning. It wouldn't do it often enough to incite replacing. Most of the time—just enough to ensure its survival—the lamp stayed on. Then it would shut off, unannounced, as if a toddler had sneaked in and found the switch. Click. This quirky personality trait was particularly irritating during nighttime reading. I'd be caught up in something good, enjoying myself, lost in the story when suddenly . . . darkness. The page was gone, the book vanished; I was yanked right out of the experience, startled away as if by magic.

Of course the book didn't *actually* vanish. The light simply turned off. It had to do with an unreliable switch; it was explicable.

So how do we explain this on-again, off-again experience most people have in their search for God? Sometimes God seems so near, but not always. Other times he seems to have gone elsewhere. It's hard on the heart and soul. I do say *seems* to, for God never really vanishes, no more than the book I was reading. He's always, always near:

Be sure of this: I am with you always, even to the end of the age. (Matthew 28:20 NLT)

Never will I leave you; never will I forsake you. (Hebrews 13:5)

In him we live and move and have our being. (Acts 17:28)

God surrounds us; we swim in God like we swim in oxygen. He is by your side right this very moment, as you read this sentence. Despite this reality—and what a wonderful reality it is—we don't always feel him near; don't have a consistent experience of his presence (some people rarely experience his presence). It can be so disheartening; I hate that rollercoaster.

But I don't think we understand what's happening. We think God either presents himself to us or doesn't, according to some rules of the spiritual game we aren't entirely sure of. So we go about our days waiting for the next appearance, like people who missed the 5:15 train and are milling about till another one arrives. Like stargazers waiting for the next shooting star.

Yet God is always here—not only around us but *within* us:

I will ask the Father, and he will give you another Advocate, who will never leave you. He is the Holy Spirit . . . he lives with you now and later will be *in you* . . . you will know that I am in my Father, and you are in me, and I am *in you*. (John 14:16–20 NLT, emphasis added)

Christ will make his home *in your hearts* as you trust in him (Ephesians 3:17 NLT, emphasis added)

And this is the secret: *Christ lives in you*. (Colossians 1:27 NLT, emphasis added)

We are never apart from God. He is both around us and within us. How much closer can he get? Why is it, then, that we don't enjoy the experience of Jesus and his resources on a more consistent basis?

Because we have a wobbly light switch inside, and the switch is belief.

ON AND OFF

I woke up this morning feeling blah for no apparent reason.

Yesterday was a good day; I slept fine during the night. But when I woke, my heart was heavy. God didn't seem to be in the house anymore. Part of me wanted to just lie there and wallow in it, give way to the low feelings for awhile, but the angels of my better nature

GET YOUR LIFE BACK

knew I needed to get up and pray. I threw off the covers (cold is not a bad motivator), went out in the living room, and slogged through my morning ritual without the feeling of his presence that I cherish. I wish I could say that I wake most mornings with an immediate, intimate connection with God, the conversation already flowing. I had a friend who would sometimes wake and see Jesus sitting on the end of her bed; wouldn't that be wonderful? But things come over us in the night—subconscious fears, failures, worries. And there is the enemy, too, a dark lion who often visits in the night. We wake to accusation, discouragement, heavy heartedness.

As the old poet George MacDonald admitted, late in his Christian life,

> Sometimes I wake, and, lo! I have forgot
> And drifted out upon an ebbing sea!
> My soul that was at rest now resteth not,
> For I am with myself and not with thee.[1]

Yep—that's pretty much how I felt. So I decided to try an experiment.

As I struggled through my prayers this morning, I chose to observe the power of belief. I gently detached from my low feelings and simply chose to believe that God was near. I basically said to my forlorn soul, *Feelings, I'm sorry you aren't well, but I'm not letting you define my experience right now. I think you are misguided. God is right here, I am his, we are close friends. I'm not sure why I feel low, but it simply isn't true.* Then I turned my attention toward God, as if he was right there next to me. *Father, thank you that you're right here. That we are good. There's nothing wrong. I simply align myself with you again today.* From this point, I carried on with my prayers.

The effect was startling. Suddenly, God was back, as if he'd reappeared, *poof*, like a genie.

Fascinated, I turned back toward my downcast feelings, and like the old lamp, the light went out of my experience. *Click*—I was alone in the room. Hating that condition, I gently detached from my feelings again, by which I mean I gave them no "say" over my interpretation of reality, the day, my experience. I ignored them, and turned back toward God: *Jesus, thank you that you are right here. You are with me, and you are in me. We are good. Click*—he was back.

I was startled by my findings. I honestly thought my feelings were a fairly decent report of reality. This was a very hopeful turn of events—my experience of God doesn't have to come and go like I thought it did.

The experiment wasn't an exercise in denial, by the way. This is exactly what the psalmist instructs us to do:

> Why, my soul, are you downcast?
> Why so disturbed within me?
> Put your hope in God,
> for I will yet praise him,
> my Savior and my God. (Psalm 42:11)

He is kind to his troubled soul, but he doesn't let it drive the bus. He gently redirects his gaze: *I understand, my dear soul, that you are not well. But God has not abandoned us. So I'm going to turn toward him, and not let you determine my reality.*

GOOD NEWS

I don't think we've admitted to ourselves just how much belief is a choice.

Some mornings you wake and feel God is near; the day looks hopeful. Next morning God seems far; the day has no color to it. For years I wrote this experience off to the ins and outs of the spiritual life, clouded by the weather of my emotions. Then Jesus began to show me something.

Innumerable times in the past several years, I'd be in a time of prayer, asking God's help or guidance with something or other, and Jesus would reply, *Believe me*. Just that—a direct command. *Believe.* So simple, yet it cut straight to the core of my problems. Either my wayward emotions had taken charge, or my circumstances had completely arrested my attention, but I was not settled in believing God. Nor was I operating from the position of believing God. *Believe.* The instruction revealed that I was caught up in my emotional state. Taking the simple command as the doorway back to experiencing God, I would simply say, "Okay—right. I believe you. I believe you." And Jesus would come again into my awareness. I was startled by how direct the connection was.

We wait to be struck by lightning. We wait for an epiphany. In our therapeutic age, we've become so self-conscious, so deeply entangled in our personal experiences, we think belief is also an experience, something we mostly feel. It is not. It is first and foremost an act of the will. A choice. Why else would Jesus handle the doubts of his dear friend Thomas with the command, "stop doubting and believe?" (John 20:27). Thomas had a decision to make in that moment, a decision he was quite capable of making, a decision our Lord was *waiting* for him to make. Thomas's experience was waiting on a choice.

Faith, or belief, can only be rewarded if it's something we've chosen. You don't reward your child for finishing their homework if you did it for them. Faith can't be rewarded if it simply falls on us from above. Belief is something we muster, set ourselves to, and *practice*. Especially when the "data" before us seems to argue against it. Our faith in God is our most precious possession, and God is committed to deepening and strengthening it:

So be truly glad. There is wonderful joy ahead, even though you must endure many trials for a little while. These trials will show that your faith is genuine. It is being tested as fire tests and purifies gold—though your faith is far more precious than mere gold. So when your faith remains strong through many trials, it will bring you much praise and glory and honor on the day when Jesus Christ is revealed to the whole world. You love him even though you have never seen him. Though you do not see him now,

you trust him; and you rejoice with a glorious, inexpressible joy.
(1 Peter 1:6–8 NLT)

I wish it were otherwise; I wish I could come to a settled place
of belief and stay there. I wish it were something poured on me from
above.

Then again, that sounds horrible. That's like asking my wife to
do all the loving for the two of us, like asking my friends to always
be the ones to sustain the friendship. I love God. I choose God. I
want to play an active role in our relationship. So this passage helps
me reinterpret that ebb and flow of belief that seems so true to all
human experience. God's not coming and going; I have choices to
make. My faith is being strengthened, deepened, purified. I've got to
move the function of belief from experience to conviction. Which is
why MacDonald could say,

> That man is perfect in faith who can come to God in the utter
> dearth of his feelings and his desires, without a glow or an aspi-
> ration, with the weight of low thoughts, failures, neglects, and
> wandering forgetfulness, and say to Him, "Thou art my refuge,
> because Thou art my home."[2]

There is a surprising temptation that visits those who have begun
to draw upon more of God, who would report a regular communion
with him. We shift the faculty of belief over onto our experience of
God for the very reason that we *do* experience him and enjoy those

frequent experiences so much. We get used to it; this becomes our norm, and we subtly shift belief onto our current awareness of God. But that's not where it belongs. Eventually, our experience will waver, and it will take belief down with it if we've tied belief to it. God wants strong, unshakable faith, so he sometimes withdraws the *experience* of his presence—not his actual presence, but the feeling of it—in order to mature us. He wants us to choose belief, *exercise* it.

MOST OF ALL

The search this book is dedicated to is for more of God in our lives as a growing, operational reality. There are a few critical things to believe in order to make this search go well. First off, we must be confident that God *wants* to give us more of himself. (Do you believe that? What are your current convictions about God wanting to give you himself?) The erosion of our soul by the world and the off-and-on experience most people have in the pursuit of God will, over time, sow seeds of doubt in our hearts that God really does want to give us himself. So let's listen to his desires and promises on the matter:

> Ask and it will be given to you; seek and you will find; knock and
> the door will be opened to you. For everyone who asks receives;
> the one who seeks finds; and to the one who knocks, the door will
> be opened. Which of you fathers, if your son asks for a fish, will
> give him a snake instead? Or if he asks for an egg, will give him a

scorpion? If you then, though you are evil, know how to give good gifts to your children, how much more will your Father in heaven give the Holy Spirit to those who ask him! (Luke 11:9–13)

And don't think he rations out the Spirit in bits and pieces. The Father loves the Son extravagantly. He turned everything over to him so he could give it away—a lavish distribution of gifts. That is why whoever accepts and trusts the Son gets in on everything, life complete and forever! (John 3:34 THE MESSAGE)

As we are asking God for a greater measure of his presence in us, we choose to ask confidently, believing that he *wants* to. This will help quite a bit.

Second, we choose to believe Christ is already within us, and we remind ourselves of this marvel. The springs of life well up from *within*. You're not looking for God to fall on you from above; you look for the upwelling of God from inside your own being! The French writer Jeanne Guyon really helped me understand this paradigm shift:

Your way to God begins on the day of your conversion, for conversion marks your soul's initial return to God . . . to find the God who has newly come to reside at the center of your being. Your spirit instructs your soul that, since God is more present deep within you . . . He *must* be sought within. And He must be enjoyed there. . . . Therefore, from the very beginning you find great joy in knowing that your Lord is within you and that you can find Him and enjoy Him in your inmost being.[3]

Now, let me pause and say that if you've never opened your heart to Jesus Christ, this would be a perfect time to do so. "Here I am! I stand at the door and knock," Jesus said. "If anyone hears my voice and opens the door, I will come in" (Revelation 3:20). This is the turning point for every human being, this invitation for Christ to come in. It goes something like this:

Jesus, thank you for coming to rescue me with your own life, death, and resurrection. Forgive me for living such an independent life, so far from you. I open my heart and my life to you now. I ask you to come in and be my Lord, my Savior, my friend.

Okay, it's important we have that covered. Because Christ now lives inside every person who has asked him to.

We are seeking a greater measure of God in us, and so we must remind ourselves that Jesus is already here, *inside* us. "This is the secret: Christ lives in you" (Colossians 1:27 NLT). We're not asking a distant and remote Jesus to stop what he's doing and travel across galaxies or even the planet to meet our request. He's already here; the resources you seek are already implanted within you, making it easier for him to rise up in greater measure within you.

Finally, we choose to believe it's happening. Do not keep checking your experience to verify whether God is cooperating. The person who keeps checking if their heart is beating will soon become paranoid about their heart skipping or murmuring or stopping altogether. Your heart is beating; you don't need to check every few minutes. *Thank you, Jesus, that you are giving me more and more of yourself* is the posture to take. God likes that posture; he likes being trusted. This posture of belief also opens your soul to let it happen.

GIVING IT A TRY

It might have seemed strange to you at first to find "believing" in a roster of soulful practices. I hope it makes sense now, because that's exactly what we do to find more of God—we *practice* belief. We exercise it.

We begin by transferring the faculty of belief from our feelings to our will. We choose to believe. This takes some getting used to, but we employ a bit of benevolent detachment from our own emotional roller coaster. Not dissociation, not denial, but the choice to believe despite whatever our current feelings may be. This is a very healthy thing to do, because our therapeutic culture has made us almost too conscious of our feelings.

My older evangelical readers will remember a little tract popular in the '70s that pictured a little train with three cars—engine, coal car, caboose. The engine was labeled Fact, the connecting car Faith, and the caboose Feeling. Some folks didn't like the simplistic connotation, but it helped many people toward a more steady life in God, myself included. Feelings are wonderful; we are looking for tangible experiences of God. But we must attach our belief onto fact and not let feelings run the show. When some new interruption presents itself into our experience—the unexpected bill, the meeting that might determine our employment, the discovery that our son or daughter has been up to unhealthy behavior—in those moments that feel ready to flip the switch of faith off and shift us into "God is not here," we say, "I believe. You are good. You are here."

I don't pretend this is easy. Your enemy is a powerful force, and he hates your love of God, hates your trust in him. So of course your faith has been assaulted over the story of your life. All the more reason to protect it like your life depends on it.

All of the practices we have explored in this book are designed to help. The Pause, because it gets you out of the madness for a moment and allows you to be present to God. You can use your One Minute Pause to repeat, "I love you. I *believe* you." Beauty helps because it reassures us of God's goodness and generosity. Memory helps; we remind ourselves that God has been faithful, and he will be faithful again. The old saints sang "Great Is Thy Faithfulness," both because it's true and also because they needed to *declare* it to be true.

Unplugging helps because the war on our attention—that daily barrage of input and media, the constant fire hose of "stuff" from Facebook, Twitter, Instagram, Google, Yahoo, and YouTube, plus the news and the texts you receive and email and memos at work— wages a war on our souls, and one of the immediate casualties is belief. We forget who we are, we forget who God is, we forget what he has spoken to us, we forget we live in a world at war. The news rarely reports on the wonderful things God is doing in the world. Evil loves to make it seem like it's winning, and it can feel that way if you spend time online. Pulling out to focus on Jesus and fix our eyes on him is healing for belief.

You'll want to have a daily proclamation of your faith. One of the creeds, perhaps. This is one of the functions of the "Daily Prayer" I pray (which you'll find in the back of this book). Those of you familiar with a liturgical worship model will now recognize the wisdom of the church for putting the Apostle's Creed in the weekly service:

> I believe in God,
> the Father Almighty,
> Creator of heaven and earth,
> and in Jesus Christ, His only Son, our Lord,
> who was conceived by the Holy Spirit,
> born of the Virgin Mary,
> suffered under Pontius Pilate,
> was crucified, died and was buried;
> He descended into hell;
> on the third day He rose again from the dead;
> He ascended into heaven,
> and is seated at the right hand of God the Father Almighty;
> from there He will come to judge the living and the dead.
> I believe in the Holy Spirit,
> the Holy Catholic Church,

the communion of Saints,
the forgiveness of sins,
the resurrection of the body,
and life everlasting.

I strongly suggest a regular recitation of what you believe, such as one of the creeds. Or write your own version. I keep mine in the front of my journal so I'll see it often and read through it. Even though I think to myself, *Yes, yes—I've read that a hundred times*, it always rescues me to recite it again.

An old saint I loved would say to himself every morning, when he woke, "God is here." Simple and so reorienting.

thirteen

THE HIDDEN LIFE OF GOD IN YOU

"I need to get among the trees," a woman told me yesterday. "I need to be among trees again."

We were sharing things that restore our souls, and for her it is trees—groves, woodlands, forests, orchards. I nodded. Walking through a forest is about my most favorite thing to do: when the day is hot but it's cool under the canopy, when the light is filtering down through the leaves in broken patterns, changing colors like the light in a cathedral coming through the stained glass high above. I love walking along slowly, silently, when the mossy soil is moist and you tread without a whisper. The wildlife doesn't seem to mind your presence; you might see a fox or pine marten, the flank of a deer slipping into the high ferns. It feels like the entire forest is one living, breathing entity.

And it is.

For centuries, fairy tales and legends told of forests with mythical powers. Many indigenous peoples held certain groves to be sacred. We moderns found them charming, perhaps, but unscientific. Along comes the thoroughly researched but equally magical book *The Hidden Life of Trees* by a German forester, Peter Wohlleben. He stumbles across an ancient stump one day, which he first took to be a ring of moss-covered stones. Looking closer, he discovers that the stump is still producing chlorophyll—something utterly impossible unless the trees around it were keeping it alive by sending it their own life. It led the forester into a series of dazzling discoveries about the interconnected life of the forest.[1]

When one tree in a forest is diseased, the other trees will send critical nutrition to it through the interconnection of the root system and fungi "network" in the forest floor, supporting the ill tree until it is well again.[2] Trees will also communicate with one another in this way. If a foreign invader like a beetle bores into one tree, that tree will send signals through the hidden connection in the humus, warning the others that an enemy has come; the forest responds by producing immune defenses, which they send up through their trunks and into their leaves.[3] Walking through a forest, the trees appear to be individuals, and they are. But there's an unseen shared life hidden from view, a connection of life and being I find beautiful and extraordinary.

This is very close to the interconnectedness God created each of us as individuals to have with him. I don't think our usual expressions of faith make this clear; they may even prevent us from seeking it.

WORDS FALL SHORT

We are pursuing a *sustaining* grace, a power, presence, life force—the daily experience of more of God in more of us. We are doing this largely through the healing and restoration of our own souls, the beautiful, besieged vessels he longs to fill.

> The God and Father of Jesus Christ could never possibly be satisfied with less than giving himself to his own! The whole history [of the human race] is a divine agony to give divine life to creatures. . . . More and more of it is for each who will receive it. . . . All the growth of the Christian is the more and more life he is receiving.[4]

The practices I've laid out for you here are means to that end—to both ends, really—healing the vessel so we may actively receive all that God is pouring forth.

Now for the main event.

Some readers will recall that Jesus used the imagery of a vine and its branches to describe the nature of connection he offers us. The branch is united with the vine, and that allows the vine to provide life in all its forms to the branch—sustenance, strength, immunity, resilience. The result for the branch is blossoming fruitfulness, abundant life. I'm afraid our familiarity with the passage, or at least the phrase "I am the Vine," has dimmed the miraculous offer: if you want, your life can become one shared existence with the Son of God, through whom all things were created, who sustains this glorious world.

Being the brilliant teacher he is, Jesus then followed up this metaphor with a second, one that ups the ante and drives home his sincerity with what was meant to be a startling comparison:

> I pray also for those who will believe in me through their message, that all of them may be one, Father, *just as you are in me and I am in you.* May they also be in us so that the world may believe that you have sent me. I have given them the glory that you gave me, *that they may be one as we are one*—I in them and you in me (John 17:20–23, emphasis added)

To be clear, Jesus prayed that we would experience the same kind of united life and being with him that he experienced with his Father. He reinforced how serious he is about this by asking his disciples to record this prayer for you, so that the startling force of it would be with us always, in black and white.

Over time, this extraordinary offer grew veiled through the language we adopted to explain Christian faith. Language tends to define, and sometimes limit, expectations. Currently, the common way to describe the essence of Christian experience in most circles would be along the lines of, "have faith in Christ." A good thing to have, faith is, but the phrase carries connotations. You can have faith without having much personal experience; you can hold to a certain religious faith and not actually know God yourself. (I've met many of these dear souls.) I have faith in my surgeon, but I don't know him at all. We certainly don't share our life together. I'm grateful for his help, but we aren't anything like best friends.

Evangelical teachers try to rectify this problem when they say things like, "Christianity is not a religion, it's a relationship." Which is closer to the truth. But union, oneness, integrated being—that is something else altogether.

I've been repeating as we go along that your soul is the vessel God fills. A basin is a receptacle: empty in itself, but it can be filled and was made to be filled. The water *inhabits* the fountain, which is a much closer metaphor. But the forest might be an even better picture; your being is porous like wood, not solid like marble. Your very being is made to be saturated with the being of God. You can have faith in God from a distance; you can have a "relationship" with Christ, but not be intimate. You can even find an intimacy with Christ, or your Father, or the Holy Spirit, and not be inhabited, interwoven, saturated.

Press your palms and fingers flat together like someone praying. Your left palm represents God, and your right palm you. This expression, I would say, is an expression of genuine intimacy. You and God are close. Now, while your palms remain pressed together, fold your fingers downward, so that the fingers of both hands become intertwined. This is an expression of deeper union, where your being and God's become intertwined. This entwining, this interlacing is what the hidden roots of the forest do. It might surprise some readers to hear me say this, but we are after much more than faith, even more than intimacy. We are after union, oneness—where our being and God's Being become intertwined. The substance of our life—our personality, our heart, our physicality, all of our experience—is filled over time to saturation with the substance of God's life.

THE COMMON CHRISTIAN EXPERIENCE

The typical progression of the Christian life presented in most church settings, Bible studies, Christian books, and conferences unfolds like this: faith, obedience, service. We begin with an encounter with Christ, perhaps in our childhood—we went to summer camp, we heard a salvation message, we attended a Billy Graham movie. We start with simple faith, a beginning. It's usually a very exciting season, whether you're eight, eighteen, or eighty-eight.

Over time—if we are maturing—simple faith moves beyond Jesus only as Savior to include Jesus as Lord. We move toward a life of obedience to this God who has saved us. We begin to clean up our act; some of our recreational activities and media choices change. We want to know and follow God's will for our life. This is a good thing; a human being cannot become what human beings were meant to be without this life of obedience.

Next comes the stage of participation: "Come and be a part of this!" We might be recruited or we might hear an inspiring message inviting us to serve. Come and teach, build orphanages, share your faith. We move from being receivers in the church environment to those who are helping out. The goal in this popular model of

Christian formation is faithful servants. We believe Christ, we obey Christ, we serve Christ in some way. I would venture to say that most dear, beautiful followers of Jesus have not been told there is anything beyond this.

Faithful servants do not enjoy a regular experience of deep intimacy with God. (I can speak candidly about this because I've counseled so many of them over the years.) They rarely, if ever, hear him speak to them personally. They are not benefiting from the restoration of their souls; inner healing would not be part of their experience. They are faithful servants, but they're pretty much stuck there.

The Good News, literally, is that there is so much more!

After we've tried the faithful servant stage for awhile, our heart cries out for something more. At some point our soul either says, *I'm out of here* and we eject from the program, or we seek a deeper experience. We discover that Jesus cares about our humanity; our heart matters to him. We discover there is healing from trauma and wounding. There is an awakening of the heart. As our heart and soul are healed (and I hope they are being healed through this book!), we find more of ourselves *available* for a genuine intimacy with God. We draw closer and closer; it is the yearning and inclination of the soul that loves God. Over time we find we are becoming the friends of God. It's a much better life, much truer to what the Gospels describe.

And there is even more.

Both the Old and New Testaments, along with the testimony of saints down through the ages, speak of union with God as the goal of our existence. In the preface to Albertus Magnus's medieval classic, *On Union with God*, the editor begins, "Surely the most deeply-rooted need of the human soul, its purest aspiration, is for the closest possible union with God."[5] My soul responds, *Yes! That's it—the closest possible union!*

However, when I look at the popular books, podcasts, sermons, and conferences being offered in Christendom, I'm struck by how rarely the topic is union with God.

They're either focused on things to do: "How to help your kids grow in their faith," or "Do this for your community to share the love of Christ," or "Take action to bring justice to the world." Or the message focuses on inspiration: "Be a better you! Live a braver life! You, too, can overcome!" There's a place for these things, of course. Absolutely. But I think they are misleading, because something else is needed first. Our energy, vitality, strength, and endurance, all virtues like patience, loving-kindness, and forgiveness—these all flow from our union with God. When the soul tries to produce any of these on its own, it tires very quickly.

The great danger for sincere people is rather surprising: "Be a good woman; be a good man." It is dangerous, not because it seems like the virtuous path, but because we're still living from our own resources. "Apart from me," Jesus warned his closest friends, "you can do nothing" (John 15:5). He said that as he was explaining the vine-branch relationship. We are cut flowers, dear reader. We need more than a vase; we need to be grafted into a vine. And so union with God, oneness of being, ought to be what we crave, what we pray for, a central part of our language, the main thing we seek.

TOWARD UNION

A beautiful writer and teacher whom I greatly respect said to a group of sincere disciples one day, "God never gives anyone more than they can handle." With all due respect, I have to say while that is a lovely and comforting thought, it simply isn't true. God is committed that his sons and daughters learn how to live a supernatural life, drawn from supernatural resources. How will he teach us to do that? He will put us in circumstances that are far beyond our natural capabilities. Dear friends, he will put you in circumstances that look a heck of a lot like your life right now.

We come to a place in our life where nothing but union with God will do. For the sake of our own humanity, our many and complex relationships, the crises that strike out of nowhere, our need for clarity and discernment, the healing of our trauma. Not to mention joy and happiness, living in that wonderful state of carefree. The practices in this book are ultimately meant to help you cultivate *union* with God—an intertwined life.

Benevolent detachment is essential. As you learn to truly "give everyone and everything to Me," practicing it as one of your dailies, it opens up space in your soul for God to fill. Otherwise, we are crammed with other stuff—the care of our suffering parents, the crisis at school last week, the partnership that just blew up, our health. Jesus upped the ante on this practice for me one day when, in a time of prayer, he added the phrase, *As if you were done. Give everyone and everything to me* as if you were done. As if I were leaving my company tomorrow. As if I were letting go of that friendship. As if I were not caring for my parents anymore. Everything. That little addition shocked my soul into realizing, *Oh—you're serious about this.*

As we mature, God asks us to release *everything*. This is not another set of losses; this is utterly relieving. Finally, our entire being can be one with God. From there we can sort the rest out.

Surrendering the Self Life is critical as well. Even dear, devoted followers of Christ can hang onto large tracts of their own inner kingdom. It looks like "Jesus and . . ." Jesus and my political passions. Jesus and this dream job I'm about to land. Jesus and getting married, having kids. The Self Life is a very sneaky thing. It's not primarily your issues with anger or anxiety; it's what's behind those things and driving them. Every morning I find I must surrender the Self Life again and then yet again during the day. I withhold no ground for myself.

HEALING YOUR UNION WITH GOD

I wrote earlier about our trip down the Snake, and the hundreds of giant spruces that had been torn up by a severe spring runoff. Hurricanes do this too; we had some gales last year that brought down many mature trees in our neighborhood, some of them hundreds of years old. I hate coming across a living tree brought down. There's nothing you can do. Torn up from its hidden connection to the life of the forest, it will soon die.

Human beings are like downed trees, scattered here and there by the hurricanes of this world. We are uprooted. This world does violence on the soul in so many ways, and I haven't spoken much at all about the kingdom of darkness and its evil powers. The primary goal of the enemy is to keep you from union with God. His puppet, the world, prevents union simply by keeping you distracted and haggard. Running on fumes. But then there are the assaults, trauma, chronic disappointment, shock, and loss—these things strike at our union with terrible force. We are pulled apart from God, down at the roots. We feel the effects, but we might not be aware of what's happening.

So it's not enough that we talk about how wonderful union can be, that we should make it a priority. That can all remain theory. We need to look into what has damaged our union with God.

I realize this is a very poignant thing I'm raising, and I want to proceed tenderly. Do you know what's damaged your soul's union with God?

Suffering in all its forms will slowly erode union, if we're not careful. As will chronic disappointment. Satan will use your suffering, or the suffering of those you love, to introduce mistrust between you and the God you love. *You see*, he whispers, *you are on your own. God's not here for you. He didn't do a thing to help.* The suffering or disappointment alone is enough to make us pull back, like a sea anemone does when you touch it. But these insidious words poison the relationship, and our union withers. We still might hang onto belief, but as we've seen, belief is not the same as saturated union. Has your suffering caused you to pull away? If we name it, we are able to come back toward God. We can choose to open up again, and ask him to heal our hearts, heal our union.

One of our nights in the African bush, I woke about 2:00 a.m. to a terrible crashing sound. A young bull elephant was pulling up sapling trees nearby, stripping them of their leaves. It was a fearsome sight, particularly by flashlight and at sixty yards. There was such violence to it I could hardly fall back asleep. This sort of violence is what trauma does to our souls. Suffering may only wither our union, but trauma will damage it, I guarantee, because trauma damages the vessel of your soul. An actual breach is formed, a rending, and of course, the enemy is there to inject into those breaches poison, feelings of having been abandoned or even betrayed by God. We must be intentional to seek the restoration of our union.

So I've found it very important to ask God to heal my union with him on a fairly regular basis, certainly after I've gone through something that felt traumatizing. Knowing I have a role to play (the door opens from the inside), I will pray something like this:

> Father, Jesus, Holy Spirit—I need you to heal our union. Heal our union, God. I give myself to you, to be one with you in everything. I pray for union and I pray for oneness. I present my entire being to you, to be one life with you. I invite your healing love and presence into the things that have hurt our union. [Be specific if you can: The loss of my daughter. The betrayal at work. My chronic back pain.] I invite your Spirit into the places where our union has been assaulted. Come and heal me here. Cleanse

these places with your blood, dear Jesus. Let your blood wash all wounding, wash away evil, cleanse every form of trauma in me. Bring your love here. I invite the light of your presence to bring healing here. I pray your glory would heal our union. May the glory of God come into the harm and damage, and restore our union. I pray to be one heart and mind again, one life, one complete union. [I will linger a moment to see if the Holy Spirit wants to show me anything specific I need to pray.] Heal our union, God; restore and renew our union. I pray for a deeper union with you, a deeper and more complete oneness. Restore our union, in Jesus's name.

(By offering this prayer I don't mean to imply that our souls are healed of trauma in one simple pass. I have seen God do this a number of times, but we need to be gracious and allow that we might need to see a counselor or seek some healing prayer ministry. This prayer is offered as a beginning. In the day-to-day wearing down of our union with God, this will restore it. In cases of more severe harm, more help is recommended.)

Remember, God works gently. He doesn't answer trauma with a forceful response; he heals through gentleness. Sometimes it can feel dramatic, but maybe only 5 percent of the time. Most of the time the union of our soul with God is something that is very gentle and life-giving. Therefore, you have to be gentle and tuned-in to be aware of it. Cultivating the Pause, and the other practices in this book, will certainly allow you to be in places that deepen union.

Then we will become those happy trees announced in Psalm 1, whose roots dwell deep down in living water; whose leaves never, ever wither; whose life is blossoming abundance season through season.

GIVING IT A TRY

Okay, then. What I want to suggest is this: the basic things we practice, the things that are at the top of our to-do list, should be things that help us find union with God. Step one is understanding that God *wants* union with you, that union is the purpose of your creation, that it's the priority. This is a good starting point; it's a massive reorientation.

Step two is presenting ourselves to God for union. I do this every day: "I present myself to you, God, for union with you." We pray for union; we ask for it. I ask for it during the One Minute Pause.

Step three (and this isn't science, folks, it's poetry; these "steps" are simply for clarity's sake) is to move toward a greater release of everything else taking up room in your soul. This is how we love the Lord our God with *all* our heart, soul, mind, and strength. "I give everyone and everything to you *for union with you.*"

As we move in and out of the various pressures and crises of life, we ask God to heal our union with him. The prayer above will help.

fourteen

THE SIMPLE DAILY THINGS

It's 5:20 p.m. on a midwinter day. The sun has almost set, and only now do I realize that not once have I even looked up at the sky today. I don't know if it's been cloudy or sunny. I don't know if the geese have been flying or if there was a beautiful sunrise. We live every moment of our lives under this gorgeous blue canopy, the dome of a great cathedral, and how seldom we enjoy it. My soul has been "gloved" today, cocooned in the artificial world.

In fact, the only reason I came outside at all is because of the injury one of our horses incurred (which I mentioned in chapter 8). It is our bay, and somehow he turned up with a serious injury to his left hip. We're not quite sure how; things take place out in the pasture beyond our understanding. They can step in a hole, or something can startle them and they jump sideways and damage a leg, in the same way it's easy for a human being to tear their knee up on a simple run. Maybe he got a whiff of lion. Now I have to come every day to where we stable them in the winter and give our bay some exercise, gently walking him around, getting him to use his muscles, keep him from going lame. It's a serious thing for a horse to go lame. Our vet thought we might have to "put him down," as the horrible expression goes. That would have been heartbreaking.

So you can bet I've come every day. At first this task was stressful, filled with worry and concern. One more thing I needed to do in an already busy week. I secretly resented it.

But as we've progressed through this book together, we've explored the healing power of beauty and nature. We've talked about the grace of pauses in our day, the kindness of transitions, our need to get outside. Right here, in what I thought was one more grievance upon an already burdened life, it turns out God had something redemptive in mind. Being forced to stop my day, come here and spend time with these horses, has been a *rescue*. Life picks up momentum like a car on downhill ice, and it's so easy to just go with it. The pace is addictive; it gives us a false sense of purpose while also relieving us of paying attention to the deeper things. God gently slowed things down for me.

I'm just standing here, letting the horses graze while I hold their halters. I'm not productive; I'm gloriously inefficient.

Only now do I notice the clouds doing the most beautiful rippled pattern all across the southern sky, like a white silk scarf blowing ever so gently in an ocean breeze but translucent, so the haze of blue comes through. A herd of deer are cautiously grazing out into the field; there's a beautiful buck among them, with a gorgeous rack of antlers. For the first time I notice that the day has a scent to it, a distinctly winter tang—that mix of dried grasses and moist cold. Icy air has a metallic taste to it, like wet aluminum. As I walk our horses along, I look down and notice the dried many-flowered asters at my feet, how they were coated in ice last night and now look like tiny crystal goblets. This evening they are serving up a communion my heart desperately needed but only realized once I got out here and settled down.

The living presence of a horse beside me, his massive warm flanks, the weather, the quiet beauty are causing me to awaken, and as I do I'm aware again of the presence of God right here with me. Part of me wants to say, "Where have you been all day?" But I know the real question is where did *I* go all day?

BAROMETERS

Several years ago a caring friend, alarmed at the number of pressures I was living under, asked me when I knew I was carrying too much. I blithely replied, "Oh, I have several barometers in my life. Our horses are one—having to come and feed them, exercise them, keeps me from self-destructing." What I said was partly true; the horses *are* a good barometer of the madness of our lives. If we're making time to see them—they are stabled near enough—it means we have reasonable pace to our days, and we are making good choices with that margin. All that's true; I simply fail to listen to my own counsel.

I haven't seen the horses for weeks, maybe a month. Not until I was forced to come daily, a rope thrown to a drowning man.

Life out there in the mad world remains what it is, spinning into greater frenzy, so we all need a quiver of gentle reminders—signs, symptoms, barometers—that let us know if we're living a sane life, healing the vessel God fills, creating opportunities for him to fill us. As I said in the introduction, this world demands a life saturated with God, and this world is the perfect storm to prevent our souls from having it. We must shepherd our heart and soul with kindness and compassion so that the springs of life may flow freely, up through the fountain of our being (Proverbs 4:23).

I know I've been sucked back into the madness when I flinch at a request for any kind of help: the text of a friend asking for my time, the email seeking some counsel. Or when Stasi shares the report of friends in crisis and everything in me wants to pull away rather than move toward them. Or when I don't even want to look at email, because I know there are demands waiting for me there. The flinch, wince, long hesitation, unhappy sigh; the avoidance, the inability to enter in—these are symptoms that we're running on fumes again.

Our capacity for relationship is such a wonderful gauge. We are created in the image of a profoundly relational God, created for relationship. Am I available for relationship? Not with everyone all the time of course—I'm not meaning the entire social network with no boundaries whatsoever, not 24/7 access. I'm talking about the people in my life: loved ones, colleagues, neighbors out walking their dogs. If I've lost the capacity for, and the *enjoyment* of relationship, I know things are deeply off in my soul.

Sugar and caffeine are always warning signs. Have I moved from enjoying them to needing them, relying on them to get me through the rest of my day? What about a simple pause? Even though I wrote the book, the One Minute Pause can be so disruptive on some days, even irritating. Yikes. If I'm hassled by a sixty-second pause, I'm deep down the drainpipe.

But there are positive barometers, too, wonderful things; these are so much better to watch. Have I seen my horses? Was I able to pay attention to what Stasi was saying this morning? Am I making room for beauty, nature, the act of simply loving God? Positive signs and reminders are better for us to watch, because these slip away before you begin to really sink in the mire. If I've reached the point that I don't want to play with my grandchildren, I'm not well. But way before that happens, I can tell how I'm doing if I'm neglecting the simple practices that bring me healing, solace, more of God. Like my evening walk.

My daily walk is a good benchmark because it's simple, accessible, and tells me whether or not I'm living realistically. I'm not talking about hours wandering through the enchanted forest (though I love that); I'm talking about a twenty-minute walk in the evening. How affirming to see this included in a list of "The Daily Routines of Geniuses," published in *Harvard Business Review*. The author compared the schedules and lifestyles of "161 painters, writers, and composers, as well as philosophers, scientists, and other exceptional thinkers" and discovered they all shared some things in common:

+ A workspace with minimal distractions
+ A daily walk (many would write in the morning, stop for lunch and a stroll, spend an hour or two answering letters, and knock off work by two or three in the afternoon)
+ A clear dividing line between important work and busywork
+ Limited social lives[1]

I know, I know, it sounds idyllic—something from a bygone era. Maybe. You can't get out for a walk? You can't cut back your social life, which in this culture means cutting down your social media and texting? Both are very doable. I love the idea of making your home or apartment a place that feels restorative to your soul. You want your "space," whatever it is, to be your sanctuary and haven, even if your neighbor loves his leaf blower.

When I got home from my Montana road trip, it was time to give this book serious attention. (I was a bit behind schedule.) But when I walked into my home office, I was struck by the fact that the visual experience before me was exactly the same as it has been for sixteen years. Same things on my desk, same view out the window, same artwork on the walls. It had gone stale long ago; I'd just gotten used to it. I needed freshness. I needed to clear out the accumulated clutter. I needed a space that corresponded to the very things I'm writing about, a space my soul felt good to be in. So I spent a few days redoing my office: moving furniture, returning to the bookcases the many volumes that had wound up stacked on the floor, shuffling off to the garage various gear that could better be stored there. Mostly what I did was simplify. I made it a space that felt quieting to walk into.

Reading for pleasure has become a good sign for me too; I had abandoned it completely. We know now that the internet is messing with our brains, making it nearly impossible to pay attention to anything for more than a flit and a flicker. When I read Nicholas Carr's experience, I winced in seeing my own:

> I began to notice that the Net was exerting a much stronger and broader influence over me than my old stand-alone PC ever had. It wasn't just that I was spending so much time staring into a computer screen. It wasn't just that so many of my habits and routines were changing as I became more accustomed to and dependent on the sites and services of the Net. The very way my brain worked seemed to be changing. It was then that I began worrying about my inability to pay attention to one thing for more than a couple of minutes. At first I figured the problem was a symptom of middle-age mind rot. But my brain, I realized, wasn't just drifting. It was hungry. It was demanding to be fed the way the Net fed it—and the more it was fed, the hungrier it became. Even when I was away from my computer, I yearned to check email, click links, do some Googling. I wanted to be *connected* . . . the Internet, I sensed, was turning me into something like a high-speed data processing machine. . . .
>
> I missed my old brain[2]

When I read that, I thought, *I miss my soul*. The world is changing our habits and routines; we need to push back. So enjoying a book or magazine has become an act of self-defense. As is time to enjoy making, and lingering, over dinner. Several times a week. Honestly, simply the ability to enjoy *anything* is a good sign to watch for.

Along with this I would add "the ability to hope and dream." Are you looking forward to your future? What are your dreaming about these days? Or are you hunkered down, braced against the world, just getting by? Let that test be a sign to you.

Maybe you simply need some carefree time on lonesome roads, the frenzy of your world fading in the rearview mirror. Don't be fooled into thinking you can't get out for awhile. There are nearly three million miles of rural roads in the US; more than one-third of all road miles are still gravel or dirt roads.[3] Helen MacDonald could find some countryside a drive from Oxbridge. When I lived in DC, the country roads of Maryland were a great solace to me. The very early morning—followed by evening—is the absolutely best time, in my opinion, to watch the beauty of the light and what it's doing in the countryside, to enjoy the long sweeping arcs and bends in the road.

Moseying allows you to practice something Dallas Willard felt was essential in this world: "You must ruthlessly eliminate hurry from your life."[4] To see an eagle perched on a snag, to hear the call of the meadowlark (do drive with the windows down when you can). I saw a fox yesterday running along the side of the road. I slowed down to watch it, and it disappeared into an irrigation pipe. I could hear his little claws clattering on the steel of the pipe, echoing in it. I saw a moose coming over the pass a few weeks ago; she had run across the road and was just disappearing into the woods when I caught my glimpse. These are the pennies from heaven Annie Dillard talks about,

> Unwrapped gifts and free surprises. The world is fairly strewn and studded with pennies cast broadside from a generous hand. . . . If you crouch motionless on a bank to see a tremulous ripple thrill on the water and are rewarded by the sight of a musk-rat kit paddling from its den, will you count that sight a chip of copper only, and go on your rueful way? It is dire poverty indeed when a man is so malnourished and fatigued that he won't stoop to pick up a penny.[5]

Or those hundred-dollar gifts of beauty God keeps leaving for us. Remember—stop and receive these gifts: *Thank you for this beauty, Father. I receive it into my soul. I receive this gift and through it your love, your goodness, your life.*

What will your barometers be? The negative ones are obvious: when you find yourself hating your political opponents, framing angry Facebook replies in your mind, wanting to run bad drivers off the road. But what's on the positive side? Is it listening to music in the evening? If so you know that when you haven't for several weeks, things are amiss.

We have a lot of dog walkers in our neighborhood, mostly out in the mornings and evenings. I've been watching this one fellow who has an odd-looking, mid-sized dog that doesn't fit any breed I'm familiar with; he looks like a loaf of bread. Cute, but he seems reluctant to participate in the walking ritual. Every time I see them, the owner is out front, arm and leash fully extended behind him. Coming along behind, moseying, not forlorn but just kind of at his own pace, is this little mutt. The owner is clearly trying to get some exercise ("get a workout in," as the saying goes, because it is something to be jammed into a frenzied life). His dog on the other hand is simply out to be out, to enjoy the world. Today the mutt had rolled over on his back on the sidewalk, paws up in the air in playful protest, while the owner was out front, arm and leash fully extended, tugging to get his companion moving. It made me laugh.

And then I realized—that's my soul; that's me and my soul. I'm trying to get my soul to come along in a way of life it just doesn't want to cooperate with. Pay attention: if it feels like you're dragging your soul along behind you, take notice. Maybe you're asking it to work at the speed of advanced technology; maybe it means you're asking it to move too quickly through the myriad challenges of your life, with no transition. It might just need to lie on its back and put its paws in the air for a few minutes.

MORE OF GOD!

Now, two little qualifications, or clarifications, to the use of barometers.

First, something is going to happen to you, may already be happening, which could really throw you for a loop without some interpretation. Augustine described the whole life of the Christian as a holy longing. Your heart is going to grow for the kingdom, more and more as you mature, which allows us to receive more and more of God and *enjoy* so much more of the life he's giving. But this can be very disorienting if you don't understand what's taking place within you. Just as you reach a place where you feel satisfied, it seems you need more. That's because your soul is expanding, which is a very good thing.

Some of the old habits, even the old comforts, just won't work anymore; some of your old relationships won't either, nor will certain religious associations. You no longer fit. We can think there's something wrong with us, when what's happening is that we are being healed toward heaven, toward Eden. As our soul is restored, it will fit less and less into the madness of this world and this hour, which, sadly, has infected Christianity quite deeply. No judgments, no need to make a scene. But you're not a moral failure because you don't fit; you're being healed. Time to move on.

The second caution comes to us through the Old Testament story of manna. The entire nation of Israel is ransomed from Egypt "with a strong hand and powerful arm, with overwhelming terror, and with miraculous signs and wonders" (Deuteronomy 26:8 NLT). Stepping through the sundered waters of the Red Sea, the people find themselves in a roundabout trek, zigzagging across the arid desert of the Sinai Peninsula (with no annual rainfall to speak of).

Masses of people wandering barren wasteland are going to die for lack of food and water in a matter of weeks, maybe days. Forty years is out of the question. So God provides his people with the bread of angels every morning. They couldn't store it, they couldn't hoard it. They had to go out each morning and gather it. And it was always there, delivered silently, gently.

Now, why did God give us this unforgettable parable?

Because no matter how much of God we've finally been able to partake of, the surprising "aha" is that we need it again tomorrow. I always thought that, for some reason, I could get to a place where I was tapped into God in such a way I didn't run out. But we need to sleep again every night; we need to drink water every day; we need to breathe again every single moment. Our life is a beautifully dependent existence, like the tree and the forest. You're not failing because you need God again tomorrow. You're not a spiritual disaster because you need so much more of him. This is the nature of things. We simply come and ask. "Give us today our daily bread" (Matthew 6:11).

We practice those things that bring us more of God.

IN CLOSING

A friend said to me this morning, "I think most people are slowly losing the war of attrition. I realize, I used to be funnier, I used to have a great sense of humor. I started thinking about it, and I see I'm just not enjoying my life like I once did."

I'm afraid it's true. The withering effects of our frenzied culture, the narrowing of mind and soul by technology, not to mention the heartbreak of the world delivered daily to smartphones, and the trauma of those in crisis around us. No time to attend to disappointments, losses, griefs. Much less cultivating precious hopes and dreams. All that's been pushed aside. Behind it all, the Great War with evil is raging, more bitter than ever. Most folks live their lives in a state of harried dullness, trench warfare, the Maginot Line. The light is fading from their eyes; their life reduced to a moment-by-moment getting by.

The enemy is frankly happy to leave them in that place. Just wear humanity down, push them into the shallows, make it so they can't possibly give God their attention and receive his graces. In that haggard, famished condition, he can then present the false gods that will bind them forever.

Dear friends, I hope you see clearly now that more of God is our greatest need, our greatest joy, our only rescue. This isn't optional. He's the source of the strength and resiliency we need for this hour, the Life that allows us to enjoy everything else in life.

So the very simple question as we close is this: What will you do, on a daily and weekly basis, to find God and receive more of him?

There are many traditional practices I didn't mention: prayer, fasting, the sacraments. But there are good books on those things.[6] There are also monastic practices like simple work. The summer I lost my dear friend, I built a log rail fence. Long hours of simple, manual labor was exactly what my soul needed. God knew that, brought it to me just in time. He will bring the things you need across your path in the time you need them too. Your soul will let you know when it's not doing well, when it needs attention, and often what it needs. Simply the fact that you've read a book—on soul care to boot—and carried through to the end reassures me that you'll do fine from here.

So let me leave you for now with a piece of advice and a blessing. The advice comes from St. Paul, who lovingly and tenderly offered this to his dear sons and daughters in the faith:

> Keep putting into practice all you learned and received from me—everything you heard from me and saw me doing. Then the God of peace will be with you. (Philippians 4:9 NLT)

I love the kindness of this encouragement. *Keep* putting into practice. It's not about perfection; it's not about being amazing. God is nowhere in the pressure to be amazing. He's waiting in the simple dailies. Just keep putting into practice the things that heal your soul and bring you more of Jesus. Then the God of peace will be with you. You'll no longer be sipping God from teaspoons; you'll learn to drink deeply from the tangible, nourishing, life-giving presence of the eternal God—Father, Son, and Holy Spirit—the fountain of living waters.

Which is my blessing:

May the Son of God, who is already formed in you, grow in you, so that for you he will become immeasurable, and that in you he will become laughter, exultation, the fullness of joy which no one can take from you.

—ISAAC OF STELLA

THE DAILY PRAYER

My dear Lord Jesus, I come to you now to be restored in you, renewed in you, to receive your life and your love and all the grace and mercy I so desperately need this day. I honor you as my Lord, and I surrender every aspect and dimension of my life to you. I give you my spirit, soul, and body, my heart, mind, and will. I cover myself with your blood—my spirit, soul, and body, my heart, mind, and will. I ask your Holy Spirit to restore me in you, renew me in you, and lead this time of prayer. In all that I now pray, I stand in total agreement with your Spirit and with all those praying for me by the Spirit of God and by the Spirit of God alone.

Dearest God, holy and victorious Trinity, you alone are worthy of all my worship, my heart's devotion, all my praise, all my trust, and all the glory of my life. I love you, I worship you, I give myself over to you in my heart's search for life. You alone are Life, and you have become my life. I renounce all other gods, every idol, and I give to you, God, the place in my heart and in my life that you truly deserve. This is all about you, and not about me. You are the Hero of this story, and I belong to you. I ask your forgiveness for my every sin.

Search me, know me, and reveal to me where you are working in my life, and grant to me the grace of your healing and deliverance and a deep and true repentance.

Heavenly Father, thank you for loving me and choosing me before you made the world. You are my true Father—my creator, redeemer, sustainer, and the true end of all things, including my life. I love you, I trust you, I worship you. I give myself over to you, Father, to be one with you as Jesus is one with you. Thank you for proving your love for me by sending Jesus. I receive him and all his life and all his work which you ordained for me. Thank you for including me in Christ, forgiving me my sins, granting me his righteousness, making me complete in him. Thank you for making me alive with Christ, raising me with him, seating me with him at your right hand, establishing me in his authority, and anointing me with your love and your Spirit and your favor. I receive it all with thanks and give it total claim to my life—my spirit, soul, and body, my heart, mind, and will.

Jesus, thank you for coming to ransom me with your own life. I love you, worship you, trust you. I give myself over to you to be one with you in all things. I receive all the work and triumph of your cross, death, blood, and sacrifice for me, through which my every sin is atoned for, I am ransomed, delivered from the kingdom of darkness, and transferred to your kingdom; my sin nature is removed, my heart circumcised unto God, and every claim being made against me is cancelled and disarmed. I take my place now in your cross and death, dying with you to sin, to my flesh, to this world, to the evil one and his kingdom. I take up the cross and crucify my flesh with all its pride, arrogance, unbelief, and idolatry [and anything else you are currently struggling with]. I put off the old man. Apply to me all the work and triumph in your cross, death, blood, and sacrifice; I receive it with thanks and give it total claim to my spirit, soul, and body, my heart, mind, and will.

Jesus, I also receive you as my Life, and I receive all the work and triumph in your resurrection, through which you have conquered sin, death, judgment, and the evil one. Death has no power over you, nor does any foul thing. And I have been raised with you to a new life, to live your life—dead to sin and alive to God. I take my place now in your resurrection and in your life, and I give my life to you to live your life. I am saved by your life. I reign in life through your life. I receive your hope, love, faith, joy, your goodness, trueness, wisdom, power, and strength. Apply to me all the work and triumph in your resurrection; I receive it with thanks, and I give it total claim to my spirit, soul, and body, my heart, mind, and will.

Jesus, I also sincerely receive you as my authority, rule, and dominion, my everlasting victory against Satan and his kingdom, and my ability to bring your Kingdom at all times and in every way. I receive all the work and triumph in your ascension, through which Satan has been judged and cast down, and all authority in heaven and on earth has been given to you. All authority in the heavens and on this earth has been given to you, Jesus, and you are worthy to receive all glory and honor, power and dominion, now and forever. I take my place now in your authority and in your throne, through which I have been raised with you to the right hand of the Father and established in your authority. I give myself to you, to reign with you always. Apply to me all the work and triumph in your authority and your throne; I receive it with thanks and I give it total claim to my spirit, soul, and body, my heart, mind, and will.

I now bring the authority, rule, and dominion of the Lord Jesus Christ and the full work of Christ over my life today: over my home, my household, my work, over all my kingdom and domain. I bring the authority of the Lord Jesus Christ and the full work of Christ against every evil power coming against me—against every foul spirit, every foul power and device. [You might need to name them—what has been attacking you?] I cut them off in the name of the Lord; I bind and banish them from me and from my kingdom now, in the mighty name of Jesus Christ. I also bring the full work of Christ between me and every person, and I allow only the love of God and only the Spirit of God between us.

Holy Spirit, thank you for coming. I love you, I worship you, I trust you. I receive all the work and triumph in Pentecost, through which you have come, you have clothed me with power from on high, sealed me in Christ, become my union with the Father and the Son, the Spirit of truth in me, the life of God in me, my counselor, comforter, strength, and guide. I honor you as Lord, and I fully give to you every aspect and dimension of my spirit, soul, and body, my heart, mind, and will—to be filled with you, to walk in step with you in all things. Fill me afresh, Holy Spirit. Restore my union with the Father and the Son. Lead me into all truth, anoint me for all of my life and walk and calling, and lead me deeper into

Jesus today. I receive you with thanks, and I give you total claim to my life.

Heavenly Father, thank you for granting to me every spiritual blessing in Christ Jesus. I claim the riches in Christ Jesus over my life today. I bring the blood of Christ once more over my spirit, soul, and body, over my heart, mind, and will. I put on the full armor of God: the belt of truth, breastplate of righteousness, shoes of the gospel, helmet of salvation; I take up the shield of faith and sword of the Spirit, and I choose to be strong in the Lord and in the strength of your might, to pray at all times in the Spirit.

Jesus, thank you for your angels. I summon them in the name of Jesus Christ and instruct them to destroy all that is raised against me, to establish your Kingdom over me, to guard me day and night. I ask you to send forth your Spirit to raise up prayer and intercession for me. I now call forth the kingdom of God throughout my home, my household, my kingdom, and domain in the authority of the Lord Jesus Christ, giving all glory and honor and thanks to him. In Jesus' name, amen.

ACKNOWLEDGMENTS

So many people to thank...

Luke Eldredge, my researcher. Dan Allender, who also provided valuable insights. Webb, my brilliant editor who always improves my work. The whole team at Nelson. My warrior-friends at Yates and Yates.

And dear Brian Hampton, to whom this book is dedicated—not just by me, but the whole team. We lost him during the creation of this work. He has gone before us. For a while.

NOTES

INTRODUCTION

1. Roger Bohn, and James Short, "Measuring Consumer Information," *International Journal of Communication* 6 (2012): 980–1000.

2. Gaurav Patki, Naimesh Solanki, and Samina Salim, "Witnessing Traumatic Events Causes Severe Behavioral Impairments in Rats," *International Journal of Neuropsychopharmacology* 17, no. 12 (2014): 2017–29, http://doi.org/10.1017/S1461145714000923; Victim Support and Child Witness Service, "Coping with Witnessing a Traumatic Event," Government of Western Australia, Department of the Attorney General, https://www.courts.justice.wa.gov.au/_files/Coping_with_witnessing _traumatic_event.pdf; Aaron Reuben, "When PTSD Is Contagious," *Atlantic*, December 14, 2015, https://www.theatlantic.com/health/archive /2015/12/ptsd-secondary-trauma/420282/; E. Alison Holman, Dana Rose Garfin, and Roxane Cohen Silver, "Media's Role in Broadcasting Acute Stress Following the Boston Marathon Bombings," *Proceedings of the National Academy of Sciences of the United States of America* 111, no. 1 (2014): 93–98, http://doi.org/10.1073/pnas.1316265110.

3. J. R. R., Tolkien, *The Fellowship of the Ring: Being the First Part of The Lord of the Rings* (New York: Ballantine Books, 1954), 34.

4. Nicholas Carr, *The Shallows: What the Internet Is Doing to Our Brains* (New York: W. W. Norton & Company, 2011), 5–9.

5. Psalm 42:7.

6. C. S. Lewis, *The Problem of Pain*, in *The Complete C. S. Lewis Signature Classics* (New York: HarperCollins, 2007), 654.

CHAPTER 1: THE ONE MINUTE PAUSE

1. Stephen E Ambrose, *Crazy Horse and Custer* (New York: Anchor, 1975), 6.
2. Thomas Merton, *The Wisdom of the Desert* (New York: New Directions, 1960), 3.

CHAPTER 2: BENEVOLENT DETACHMENT

1. St. Augustine, *Expositions on the Book of Psalms*, in *A Library of Fathers of the Catholic Church* (London: F. & J. Rivington, 1857), 167.
2. Ann Chanler, "Mindfulness Meets Enmeshment: Disentangling Without Detaching with Embodied Self-Empathy as a Guide," *Spirituality in Clinical Practice* 4, no. 2 (2017): 145–51.

CHAPTER 3: DRINKING BEAUTY

1. Elaine Scarry, *On Beauty and Being Just* (Princeton, NJ: Princeton University Press, 1999), 23–25.
2. Jake Miller, "Better by Design," *Harvard Medicine* (Winter 2015), https://hms.harvard.edu/magazine/assembled-care/better-design.
3. Scarry, *On Beauty and Being Just*, 50.
4. Scarry, 69.
5. Scarry, 47.
6. Scarry, 33.
7. Scarry, 33.

CHAPTER 4: SIMPLE UNPLUGGING

1. Elizabeth Hoge, David Bickham, and Joanne Cantor, "Digital Media, Anxiety, and Depression in Children," *Pediatrics* 140, supp. 2 (November 2017), https://pediatrics.aappublications.org/content/140/Supplement_2/S76; University of Pennsylvania, "Social Media Use Increases Depression and Loneliness, Study Finds," Science Daily, November 8, 2018, https://www.sciencedaily.com/releases/2018

/11/181108164316.htm; Sarah Fader, "Social Media Obsession and Anxiety," Anxiety and Depression Association of America, November 2018, https://adaa.org/social-media-obsession.

2. Matthew B. Crawford, *The World Beyond Your Head: On Becoming an Individual in an Age of Distraction* (New York: Farrar, Straus & Giroux, 2016), 8–9.

3. Zenith, "Media Consumption Forecasts 2017," Publicis Media, https://www.zenithmedia.com/product/media-consumption-forecasts-2017/.

4. Roger Bohn, and James Short, "Measuring Consumer Information," *International Journal of Communication* 6 (2012): 980–1000.

5. Nicholas Carr, *The Shallows: What the Internet Is Doing to Our Brains* (New York: W. W. Norton & Company, 2011), 5–9.

6. Carr, *Shallows*, 114–43.

7. Carr, 220–22.

8. Seth Godin, "Mobile Blindness," Seth's Blog, March 21, 2018, https://seths.blog/2018/03/mobile-blindness.

9. Crawford, *World Beyond Your Head*, ix.

10. Susan Weinschenk, "Why We're All Addicted to Texts, Twitter and Google," *Psychology Today*, September 11, 2012, https://www.psychologytoday.com/us/blog/brain-wise/201209/why-were-all-addicted-texts-twitter-and-google.

11. Asurion, "Tech-Tips," https://www.asurion.com/connect/tech-tips.

CHAPTER 5: KINDNESS TOWARD OURSELVES

1. C. S. Lewis, *God in the Dock: Essays on Theology and Ethics* (Grand Rapids: Wm. B. Eerdmans, 1972), 193.

2. Rainer Maria Rilke, "Roman Fountain," *New Poems*, trans. Len Krisak (Suffolk, UK: Boydell & Brewer, 2015), 125–26.

CHAPTER 6: ALLOWING FOR TRANSITIONS

1. Robert C. Ruark, *Horn of the Hunter: The Story of an African Safari* (Huntington Beach, CA: Safari Press, 1996), 2, 36.

2. Gerald G. May, *The Awakened Heart* (San Francisco: HarperOne, 1993), 3–4.

CHAPTER 7: GET OUTSIDE

1. Robert M. Pirsig, *Zen and the Art of Motorcycle Maintenance: An Inquiry Into Values* (New York: HarperCollins, 2006), 4.
2. Neil E. Klepeis et al., "The National Human Activity Pattern Survey (NHAPS): A Resource for Assessing Exposure to Environmental Pollutants," *Journal of Exposure Analysis and Environmental Epidemiology* 11, no. 3 (May–June 2001): 231–52.
3. Gerard Manley Hopkins, "God's Grandeur," in *Poems and Prose* (London: Penguin Classics, 1985), 27, line 1.
4. Hopkins, "God's Grandeur," 27, lines 5–8.
5. Hopkins, 27, lines 9–14.
6. Helen Macdonald, *H is for Hawk* (New York: Grove Press, 2016), 3.
7. Macdonald, *H is for Hawk*, 5–6.
8. Macdonald, 8–9.
9. Vincent van Gogh, "Letter to Emile Bernard, from St. Remy, Beginning of December, 1889," in *Letters of Vincent van Gogh*, ed. Mark Roskill (London: Penguin Group, 1996), 470.
10. Scott Yorko, "The Science of Why You Love the Wilderness," *Backpacker*, June 14, 2017, https://www.backpacker.com/news-and-events/science-of-why-you-love-the-wilderness.
11. C. S. Lewis, *Miracles* (San Francisco: HarperOne, 2015), 266.

CHAPTER 8: REMEMBERING WHO YOU LOVE

1. Henry Van Dyke, "The Hymn of Joy" (1907).

CHAPTER 9: SURRENDERING THE SELF LIFE

1. Dorothy Sayers, *The Other Six Deadly Sins* (London: Methuen and CO, 1943), 19–20.
2. Alice G. Walton, "6 Ways Social Media Affects Our Mental Health," *Forbes*, June 30, 2017, https://www.forbes.com/sites/alicegwalton

/2017/06/30/a-run-down-of-social-medias-effects-on-our-menta
l-health.

3. Joel Stein, "How Trolls Are Ruining the Internet," *TIME*, August 18,
2016, http://time.com/4457110/internet-trolls/.

4. Stein, "How Trolls Are Ruining the Internet."

5. Psalm 37:4; Proverbs 4:23.

6. C. S. Lewis, "Two Ways with the Self," in *God in the Dock* (Grand Rapids:
Wm. B. Eerdmans, 2014), 210–11.

7. C. S. Lewis, *The Voyage of the Dawn Treader* (San Francisco:
HarperCollins, 1994), 92.

8. Lewis, *Voyage of the Dawn Treader*, 108–9.

9. George MacDonald, *Unspoken Sermons* (London: Alexander Strahan,
1867), 366–67.

10. Sayers, *Other Six Deadly Sins*, 22.

CHAPTER 10: CARING FOR NEGLECTED PLACES IN YOUR SOUL

1. Society for Human Resource Management, "2016 Paid Leave in the
Workplace," SHRM, October 6, 2016, https://www.shrm.org/hr
-today/trends-and-forecasting/research-and-surveys/pages/2016-paid
-leave-in-the-workplace.aspx.

2. Mark Twain, *Chapters from My Autobiography* (Oxford: Benediction
Classics, 2011), 24.

3. Aaron Reuben, "When PTSD Is Contagious," *Atlantic*, December 14,
2015, https://www.theatlantic.com/health/archive/2015/12/ptsd
-secondary-trauma/420282/.

4. Karyn Hall, "Self-Soothing: Calming the Amygdala and Reducing the
Effects of Trauma," PsychCentral, April 4, 2012, https://blogs.psychcentral
.com/emotionally-sensitive/2012/04/self-soothing-calming-the-amgydala/.

CHAPTER 11: THE GIFTS OF MEMORY

1. Meister Eckhart, *Meditations with Meister Eckhart*, trans. and ed.
Matthew Fox (Santa Fe, CA: Bear, 1983), 129.

2. C. Bushdid et al., "Humans Can Discriminate More Than 1 Trillion Olfactory Stimuli," *Science* 343, no. 6177 (March 2014): 1370–72, http://doi.org/10.1126/science.1249168.

3. Jack Turner, *Teewinot: A Year in the Teton Range* (New York: Thomas Dunne Books, 2000), 140–41.

CHAPTER 12: BELIEVE

1. George MacDonald, *Diary of an Old Soul* (Minneapolis: Augsburg Publishing, 1975), January 3, lines 1–4.

2. George MacDonald, "The Child in the Midst," in *Unspoken Sermons* (London: Alexander Strahan, 1867), 24–25.

3. Jeanne Guyon, *Union with God* (Sargent, GA: SeedSowers, 1981), 1.

CHAPTER 13: THE HIDDEN LIFE OF GOD IN YOU

1. Peter Wohlleben, *The Hidden Life of Trees: What They Feel, How They Communicate: Discoveries from a Secret World* (Munich: Ludvig Verlag, 2015), 1–2.

2. Wohlleben, *Hidden Life of Trees*, 15, 18.

3. Wohlleben, 8–10.

4. George MacDonald, *Unspoken Sermons* (London: Alexander Strahan, 1867), 300–301.

5. Albertus Magnus, *On Union with God* (New York: Continuum International, 2000), 9.

CHAPTER 14: THE SIMPLE DAILY THINGS

1. Sarah Green Carmichael, "The Daily Routines of Geniuses," *Harvard Business Review*, March 19, 2014, https://hbr.org/2014/03 /the-daily-routines-of-geniuses.

2. Nicholas Carr, *The Shallows: What the Internet Is Doing to Our Brains* (New York: W. W. Norton & Company, 2011), 16.

3. Department of Transportation, Federal Highway Administration, "County Road Miles: State by State," Research Division, National

Association of Counties (2008): 1–2; Department of Transportation, Federal Highway Administration, "Public Road Length—2013: Miles by Functional System: Table HM-20, HM-10, HM-12, HM-15, VM-202," https://www.fhwa.dot.gov.

4. Dallas Willard, quoted in John Ortberg, *Soul Keeping: Caring for the Most Important Part of You* (Grand Rapids: Zondervan, 2014), 20.

5. Annie Dillard, *Pilgrim at Tinker Creek* (New York: Harper Collins, 2009), 17.

6. See *The Spirit of the Disciplines* by Dallas Willard and *Celebration of Discipline* by Richard Foster.

ABOUT THE AUTHOR

John Eldredge is a bestselling author and counselor. He is also president of Wild at Heart, a ministry devoted to helping people discover the heart of God and recover their own hearts in God's love. John and his wife, Stasi, live near Colorado Springs, Colorado. To learn more, visit wildatheart.org.

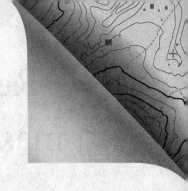

Finishing this book is only the beginning.

Continue your journey at
WildAtHeart.org

Weekly Podcasts

Video & Audio Resources

Prayers We Pray

Live Events

Download the **Wild at Heart App**.

Recover your masculine heart.

A six-session film series featuring the teaching of John Eldredge and the stories of men pursuing their warrior hearts through God's invitation of battle, adventure, and beauty.

▶ Stream for free at

WildAtHeartExperience.com

Restore your feminine heart.

Through personal stories of women and Stasi Eldredge's teachings, this six-session film series reveals every woman's longing to be loved, play an irreplaceable role in a great adventure, and bring life and beauty to the world.

▶ Stream for free at

CaptivatingExperience.com

Experience the
One Minute Pause App
on your phone today.

"I've developed an app to help you practice the Pause.
It's the beginning of a new way of living.
Your soul is going to thank you."

PauseApp.com

The *Get Your Life Back* Video Series

FOR SMALL GROUP OR INDIVIDUAL USE

If you've enjoyed this book, now you can go deeper
with the companion video series and study guide!

In each of the six sessions, John Eldredge introduces simple
practices to help restore your soul. The study guide includes
video notes, group discussion questions, and personal
study and reflection materials for between sessions.

**Available now at your favorite bookstore,
or streaming video on StudyGateway.com.**